From My Mother's Hands

Hands

Remembrances and Recipes From Texas Women

Susie Kelly Flatau

Republic of Texas Press

Plano, Texas

Library of Congress Cataloging-in-Publication Data

Flatau, Susie Kelly.
   From my mother's hands : remembrances and recipes from Texas women /
   Susie Kelly Flatau.
      p.   cm.
   Includes index.
   ISBN 1-55622-786-8 (pbk.)
   1. Mothers and daughters—Texas.   2. Parent and adult child—Texas.
   2. Cookery, American. I. Title.
   HQ755.86 .F57   2000
   306.874'3—dc21   00-032553
                                                  CIP

Printed in the United States of America

ISBN 1-55622-786-8
10 9 8 7 6 5 4 3 2 1
0005

All inquiries for volume purchases of this book should be addressed to Wordware Publishing, Inc., at 2320 Los Rios Boulevard,
Plano, Texas 75074. Telephone inquiries may be made by calling:

(972) 423-0090

For Mama

1932 - 1990

Katie Mae and Susie Kelly

"I think we have to remember that these are not just sweet and nice stories, but that they are a whole history, a whole legacy."

—Teresa Palomo Acosta

Contents

Contents

Daughters	*Mothers*	

Preface

We enter this world in a state of innocence and hope to leave it having attained wisdom, and in between these events there are two factors that strongly shape our quests—life occurrences and mentors. And so it is that *From My Mother's Hands* is a work inspired by Texas women who share the intimate moments and positive influences of their first mentors—their mothers. Indeed, this work is at its core a mosaic cemented together with words and images that express the lessons and stories these daughters have harvested from a collective matriarchy.

The first step for the book was to identify the interviewees. That task alone proved daunting, for how was I to narrow down the field? How was I to select one woman over another? Furthermore, how was I to retell the "mother-stories" without bias or interpretation? Fortunately, I did not have to search long for the answer as my inner voice rose to remind me of the existence of the "Everywoman." And with that clarity, I started to work.

Little did I know I would fall so deeply in love with these daughters and mothers, but I did. Humbled by their strong relationships, I found that while each woman has her own voice and heritage, there is a connectedness shared by all. Societal parameters drawn about the diverse lives and backgrounds of these women were erased as I glimpsed the beauty of their commonalities and differences. Where one daughter would appear similar to her mother, the next would prove opposite. Where one daughter would speak of a fun-loving mother, the next would describe a stern matron. And where one daughter would applaud her mother as eclectic, the next would praise hers as traditional.

There existed such varied elements in the textures of their words that I came to understand that one cannot and should not compare one's matriarch to the next. Ultimately I came to know that *From My Mother's Hands* serves not as a definition but rather as a celebration of the woman who tends her brood.

Within the book's framework one cannot ignore the historical snippets that when basted together become part and parcel of the women's lives; however this work does not attempt to record history per se. Instead it strives to chronicle legacies of life lessons, intimate moments, work ethics, family, loss, and so forth.

Strict efforts were made to retain the daughters' authentic voices by crafting edited, first-person narratives from taped interviews. Many recipes from the mothers were selected by the daughters; some reflect an earlier family lineage, and a few are simply favorite recipes from a daughter's files. Photographs were submitted by each daughter at her own discretion. Journal topics appearing in the back of the book are ones I use in workshops, classes, and interviews. This list, much like a tribe's fire starter, will hopefully ignite your desire to record personal thoughts, questions, and reflections about the matriarch—or matriarchs—in your own life.

—Susie Kelly Flatau

Acknowledgments

I lost my mother to cancer in 1990, and it was at that time I knew I would someday write this book. Although our mother/daughter relationship had been a rocky one during my thirty-eight years on this planet, I realized that after her passing what played upon my eyelids were the happy times, the memorable moments. And so it is that my mother's spirit traveled with me as I interviewed the beautiful women who shared their stories for this work. Mama, this book is for you.

I believe we are blessed with Earth angels to accompany us through life, and two of my most treasured angels are Jack, my husband, and Jenni, my daughter. From them I have received strength and encouragement. From them I have received understanding and forgiveness. And most importantly, from them I have received unconditional love. Jack and Jenni, I give you my love without any strings attached.

When I was ten years old, another of my angels—my brother Gary —came into my life, and for nearly forty years he and I have enjoyed a unique relationship as siblings, caretakers, friends, and advisors. Gary, you are dear to my heart.

Then there is the guardian angel who has been in my life since 1984—Mrs. Kay Morris. Although we have never lived in the same town, we have grown a friendship for sixteen years through letters and phone conversations. I can only hope she knows how important she is to me as a constant voice of reason, inspiration, and support. Mrs. Morris, you are so like my garden.

I thank Dianne Stultz, Vice President, Republic of Texas Press, for her objective and gentle nature and her editorial input. I thank Ginnie Bivona, Acquisitions Editor, for believing in and supporting my dream of writing this book. I thank Martha McCuller, Graphic Designer, for the creative spirit surrounding the words of these beautiful daughters. I thank Cathy Tindle, Marketing Director, for always being there to fill orders and answer questions with a wonderful sense of humor and patience.

Teresa Palomo Acosta

poet; educator

Sabina Palomo Acosta and Teresa Palomo Acosta

Sabina Palomo Acosta

b. 1914

This ring is my mother's first wedding band from my father. I have loved it since I was a child, so if I had to select a favorite concrete gift—the other gifts from Mother are more abstract, more spiritual—I would select this one.

I ASKED MY MOTHER if I could have this ring, and before my father died she gave it to me. For years I've known it's the only thing I wanted to keep, so when I put it on I feel a closeness, a strong link with my mother and father, who were married for fifty-five years. I think of the durability of their relationship and the solidity of being who I am because of them.

At around four years old Mother left what would have been a very different life in Mexico and came to this country as part of the Mexican Revolutionary movement. Her father was a ranch foreman, but when the revolution was beginning the owner handed him some money to leave. For a while they lived in hotels, then later they came to the States. Their lives

1

Sabina Palomo Acosta and baby Teresa, circa 1949 or 1950

were transformed as they became the proletariat, the poor and working class.

Mother went to work in the fields at the age of five. Her family's route basically started in Crystal City where they worked with spinach. Next they'd go to the Nueces area to hoe cotton and after that to West Texas to work the cotton harvest. Then they'd make their way back to Crystal City, so it was a year-round circuit of working the fields. My mother thinks it might have been a combination of her mother contracting tuberculosis—they didn't really know since there were no doctors to see them—and too many children and their living conditions, but on their way to West Texas one time, her mother died. But it's only been in the last few years that she has talked to me about the circumstances surrounding her mother's death.

My mother, who is principally monolingual Spanish, attempted schooling for a short time but only went for a flash, for a moment, so the little bit of English she learned was by hearing. Then when she married my father—who taught himself English by reading newspapers—she lived mostly in a Spanish-speaking world and didn't know much of what was going on outside of it. I think his role in some ways was to negotiate their world, and she had his protection in the sense that it gave her confidence she could do certain things even though she didn't know English.

When my father started working for the railroad, he told Mother she would never have to work in the fields again. That allowed her to retire from field labor and be a full-time mother. Now that's opposite of what many women sometimes struggle with, but for Mother that was a great release because she was no longer under the thumb of someone telling her to go chop cotton, to go pick up cotton. For years my father had to live away from home during the week because of work and Mother basically managed the whole household. So in her tenacity she never allowed being monolingual to interfere with what she wanted to do with her life. It was a hard life in some ways with four children and a husband to look after, but it was stability, and she gained this confidence of having made her way in the world by using her common sense and being frugal.

When I was about three-and-a-half years old, Mother contracted tuberculosis and had to go to a hospital in Tyler. I remember the day she left—where she was sitting and what it felt like to be wrenched from her arms because I didn't want her to go. We children couldn't go into the hospital, so during the fourteen months she was there I remember getting to see her only once and then she could only wave to us from a distance. During that time she didn't get well, and it took courage to endure months in a hospital and not make progress. Then one day my mother told my father to come pick her up because she had grown weary of feeling helpless. Ultimately she was healed, I think by her own faith and by being home, and that was a lifesaver for me.

I was possessive of her since I was at that age where I wanted her just for me, and it gave me time with her before I went to first grade. Mother always gave me time on my own and allowed me to play by myself. When I was about eleven years old, I more or less decided to become a writer, and Mother knew that what she could do for me was maintain a peaceful household so I could tap into my creativity. To this day when I'm with her and it's just us, she'll peek into the kitchen in the evening when it's quiet and ask, "Are you writing?" If I say yes, she'll go back into the living room and let me write.

I think her legacy for me will be she helped me become a writer. She gave me the quiet time and she gave me her legacy by telling me her stories and letting me put those stories down in some way. So for me she was the one who let my writing happen in a way that a school, a formal education, cannot do. She allowed the spontaneous Teresa, the imaginative Teresa to grow up to be a

Sabina Palomo Acosta.
Photo taken before her marriage at age 28

writer, and that is her legacy. She set me down on this road. She sharpened my pencils and handed them to me. So for me her legacy is that she's sort of a point of departure for me being a writer and turning to stories and poems as a way of remembrance and preservation. If I create a poem about the family, it is her ripples that are coming out of that.

What I would love to do to honor her is make sure I retell her stories in a truthful way. Her generation's stories teach how people can transform a difficult life by working hard, how these women can stand up and not be bent over. There is a need to remember that the women who ground corn didn't just sit on their knees but also stood up, and these things won't be remembered unless people know about them through books and poems, through history and research.

Writers are always borrowing things, and many of my poems would not exist if not for her. The gift of her story has allowed me to learn about her own life story, and what I am discovering is she has given me examples in her day-to-day living about perseverance and tenacity. Interestingly Mother has never read my poem "My Mother Pieced Quilts"—which essentially describes her sitting on the floor and gathering pieces of cloth then putting them together—and when I was recently asked how I felt about that, I explained that when she is present in any of my works it's because she has lived those things. Mother's own quilting was utilitarian, solely for the family, and my impression is that a lot of Chicana women did that.

I can see her hands as she quilted, and I have another image of her hands. Very often in the Mexicana tradition parents bless a child when they leave the home, and whenever I leave my mother's, I always look in my rearview mirror and watch her use her hand to bless me in the air. The other day I was thinking about the warmth of my mother's touch and the scent of her lipstick and talc-like perfume, and I know I am thankful for just her presence.

My mother negotiated at least three worlds. The world of a Mexicana woman working in the fields and struggling with ethnicity; the world of a wife and negotiating that terrain; the world of a mother knowing when to be nurturing and when to be stern.

My mother cooked by intuition, taste, and touch. So these two recipes are approximations. When you try them, tasting along the way is of paramount importance for the first one, and trial and error is the way to reach the summit of the second one.

Capirotada

> Toasted bread, torn into random-size pieces
> Dashes of cinnamon
> 1 - 1½ c. pecans
> 1 - 1½ c. grated mild yellow cheese
> 1 - 1½ c. raisins
> ⅔ - 1 c. light brown sugar
> Lukewarm water

In a large, round, and moderately deep pan with a lid add at least three layers of the above ingredients. Add lukewarm water in between layers and on top of entire concoction. Make more layers if you want a larger version.

Place lid on the pan and cook *capirotada* on the stovetop over a low-to-medium heat for approximately 30 minutes or until mixture is soft and all water is absorbed. Add water as necessary during cooking time.

Tortillas de Harina

I grew up having tortillas de harina with everything. By the way, my father usually made our rolling pins from wood to my mother's specifications, and they lasted for years. I continue to make tortillas with one of the last ones my father made for my mother. She has recently retired from decades of cooking, wisely passing on the tortilla-making tradition to the next generation.

> 2 c. white flour
> ½ - 1 tsp. salt (to taste)
> 1 tsp. baking powder
> ¼ c. vegetable oil
> Lukewarm water

Mix together dry ingredients by hand in any order. Add the vegetable oil by hand. Make a funnel in the mixture with your hand and add the lukewarm water gradually, kneading the mixture as you do by hand. Add enough water so that the dough comes together but is not sticky. Remove dough from mixing bowl and knead for a minute or two on floured surface. Form semi-flat balls of tortilla dough the size that fits comfortably in your palm—neither too large nor too small. Bring rolling pin down on tortilla dough with some pressure. Roll them out on a lightly floured surface with rolling pin. Roll them as round as possible. Transfer tortilla to a preheated cast-iron griddle. Tortillas should be cooked on medium heat. Turn over after they have an array of brown freckles on one side; turn them once again. Tortillas do not require much cooking time and can easily burn if you're not careful. Transfer tortillas to a plate with a medium-size soft cloth on its surface. Make sure you cover tortillas with part of the cloth as you drop each onto the plate.

Teresa Palomo Acosta

WALKING TO THE LBJ LIBRARY on the University of Texas campus in Austin, I experienced nervous anticipation about the upcoming interview with Teresa Palomo Acosta. Her poetry had been a part of my high school English teaching curriculum for years, and her poem "My Mother Pieced Quilts" had served as a word mosaic to introduce a year-long analogy that would be applied to the study of American literature—that each American writer, much like the quilt-making mother in Teresa's poem, is the "river current . . . the caravan master at the reins" who offers learners "October ripened canvases" that are "positioned, balanced, then cemented" together.

To now have the honor of meeting Ms. Acosta reinforced a belief that life is good. My steps quickened and before long Teresa and I sat in an empty room and she began her tales. This thoughtful woman spoke with tenderness about the matriarch who nurtured her. She tapped into her intuitive self to share the poignancy and pathos of her mother's experiences and influences. Throughout the interview, this fire keeper who perpetuates her family legacy proved that in person—as well as on the printed page—Teresa Palomo Acosta is a poet of the heart and of life.

Teresa Palomo Acosta
Photo courtesy of Mary Bruton, MKB Photography

Teresa in 1974 received a degree in Ethnic Studies from the University of Texas and from there pursued her love of people and story. As a program advisor she managed the Distinguished Speakers Series at her alma mater before moving on to receive an M.S. degree in Journalism from Columbia University in New York.

A return to Austin, Texas, resulted in roles as a part-time reporter and assistant editor for the *Texas Observer* and instructor and administrator for St. Edward's University. Other stints included working for the Texas Higher Education Coordinating Board as director of student retention services, the Texas State Historical

Teresa Palomo Acosta with doll "Cubby," the last of two store-bought dolls she ever had

Association as research associate in Mexican American history, the Center for Mexican American Studies as an adjunct lecturer and visiting fellow, and AmeriCorps as a literacy tutor to predominantly Spanish-speaking students.

And all the while she continued to create and write. The list of literary publications is too long to catalog, but suffice it to say her works have reached a multitude of people through journals, anthologies, literature textbooks, poetry chapbooks, and newspapers. Teresa has also produced works for drama and dance theater. And for her creative efforts she has reaped many awards.

However, this woman of words also reaches out to the community with action. She has served as a consultant on Mexican American women's issues, assisted AmeriCorps with community engagement and education, and volunteered with St. Austin's Catholic Church homeless youth food program and the UT-Austin chapter of Habitat for Humanity.

After all was said and done, I sat in my truck letting the depth and beauty of the interview filter into my mind and knew that Teresa Palomo Acosta, much like her mother, is a woman piecing quilts—legacy quilts.

Debbie Agbottah, Loretta Edelen, and Cheryl Sawyer

systems analyst IV; institutional research manager; director, corporate and foundation relations, KLRU-TV

(All three Delco daughters were interviewed at one time; no distinction is made to identify each individual speaker in the transcript so as to present one unified voice.)

Debbie Agbottah, Wilhelmina Delco, Cheryl Sawyer, Loretta Edelen, youngest grandchild

Wilhelmina Ruth Fitzgerald Delco

b. 1929

Mother has a strong sense of faith and has always maintained a strong belief that God will see us through. Her big saying is, "When God closes a door, he opens a window," and that is how she has lived her life.

WHAT DO I RESPECT MOST about our mom? I think the loving and the caring and just the encouragement for all of us to be able to pay attention to that little voice in ourselves. And of course I respect her whole

Wilhelmina Delco as Speaker Pro Tempore, 1991
Photo courtesy of Texas House of Representatives

sense of family and community. She's always maintained a sense that it doesn't matter what we do, she's always there for us. And I admire that she is willing to say what's on her mind and to speak her piece. There are a lot of people who will sit back and not say anything or just let things slide, but she is always willing to cut to the chase and because of that I think she has always shown courage.

Mother is dynamic in the fullest sense of the word, not only because of her multitude of talents but also because of her ability to focus on whatever the issue is at the time. She is able to identify when something needs attention then to focus on it and maintain that focus. When she was in the House of Representatives, I remember she had a picture on the wall of a little black child with one tear coming down his face, just as a reminder of what she was there for. She just has this dynamic love of life and people as well as a strong commitment to bring out the best in everything and everybody she touches. Expounding on that, I sometimes don't think she realizes the immense impact she has had on a lot of lives. People will often come up to me and say, "When I was in need, I would go to your mom and she would always be willing to help out. She was really always there for me." So it was seeing and being aware of her day-to-day interaction with people as well as her interaction with me and my sisters that naturally led me to understand you must do the right thing.

Another term for Mother would be courageous because she will get right out there in whatever she believes in and encourage people to gravitate toward all the really good things. She has this incredible compassion that is strong enough to take up causes and try to dramatically improve the quality of life circumstances for people. Anytime she speaks, she does not speak from a text, no, she thinks about who the audience is and what the issues are, and she gets in front of that audience and delivers an incredible message. She has this phenomenal gift of words to speak from her deep compassion and courage about whatever the issue is. It is such a gift.

You could also say Mother has determination because when you look at every aspect of what she has done, she has always been determined to achieve whatever the goal is she has in mind. It doesn't matter what distractions occur along the way because she's determined to maintain a positive attitude so she can stick with whatever her challenge or cause is until it's done. Along with that, I would say Mother has a lot of integrity. I remember that before I left for college one of her comments was "Whatever you do, make sure it is okay for your actions to be the headline in the morning paper or a lead story on the six o'clock news. Whatever you do, make sure it is something you would be proud for the rest of the world to know about." So again, she is always acting out of integrity, always acting in support of where you come from.

And I don't think it dawned on me until I was grown up that she was always there as a mother. I mean she was there when all of us got home from school. Her meetings outside the house really didn't interfere with her making sure the homework was completed or jobs were finished. So growing up, everything was focused on the family. Everything came second to making sure dinner was on the table, second to making sure all problems were solved. Not to mention that she made all the outfits we three girls wore. People sometimes would tease us about being like the kids in *The Sound of Music* because we'd all have matching outfits, but whatever she sewed was gorgeous and always in vogue. So when everybody else was having all those power lunches or power drinks or power dinners, Mother was doing the power family thing.

Education was emphasized to such a great extent in our family. When we were little we'd go to the library religiously and check out tons of books, then every day right

Wilhelmina as a toddler

before naptime we'd have story hour. We could select the books and Mom would read, and a lot of the time many of the neighborhood kids would come and we'd have Popsicles, so it was everybody's favorite time of day. I know that education and love of learning stemmed from our mother—actually both parents—and all the ways they integrated education and learning and knowledge into our lives as a joyful kind of thing. They had such high levels of expectation for what we were supposed to accomplish, so when we got to school it wasn't something to really stop and think about, it was just something you did.

Mother's mantra these days is the importance of family. When we get together there are at least five or six exciting discussions going on at the same time about what needs to happen here or what needs to be done, and there is just this loving activity and sharing. We've obviously grown up in a solid, strong home and been blessed with loving, adoring parents who made sure we not only had a religious foundation but that we also had a sound academic foundation. Mother has always been consistent and maintained a certain level of integrity about everything she does, so it is only reasonable that she is always the first one we go to for comfort or for support.

We really like to think about our mother's courage, because for her to go into all the different stages of life and to get to know people and to try things—regardless of the climate or traffic—just to listen to the people and to respect them, that can only be the strength of character we could all hope to realize.

Stewed Chicken

Large fryer or stewing hen
Seasoned lite salt to taste
Flour
½ onion
½ green pepper
1 stalk celery, cut up
Water
Canola oil

Cut up one large fryer or hen in serving pieces; season with seasoned salt. Cover with flour. Brown in canola oil (just enough fat to brown). Add onion, green pepper, and celery. Brown. Add water to cover. Bring to boil. Turn to low and simmer for about 1 hour until tender.

Quickie Tuna Casserole

Place 2 cans of tuna in casserole dish. Add 1 can of whole kernel corn. Combine 1 can of cream of mushroom soup with a half can of water. Pour soup over tuna and corn mixture. Heat in 350-degree oven. Cover top with grated cheese and serve.

Quickie Tuna with Chow Mein Noodles

Add 2 cans of tuna to 1 can of cream of mushroom or cheese soup. Mix and warm until well blended. Serve over chow mein noodles (canned). Serve with salad.

Debbie Agbottah, Loretta Edelen, and Cheryl Sawyer

Libraries offer a sanctuary away from the noise of day-to-day living. Simply walk through their doors and you can discover the world at your fingertips. It was in such a place that Wilhelmina Delco's

Cheryl Sawyer, Debbie Agbottah, Loretta Edelen, 1999

daughters—Debbie Agbottah, Loretta Edelen, and Cheryl Sawyer—agreed that their mother's heart and soul are special places and her guidance and love have provided a lifetime sanctuary for them.

All three women were unique yet connected; keeping this in mind, I sat before the computer to begin this piece when my thoughts wandered to one word—garland. To paraphrase its definition, a garland is a wreath—of leaves, flowers, trinkets, etc.—that can be worn about the head as a symbol of victory or honor. It was clear to me this word described these three women—victorious in their lives and bestowing honor upon their mother.

Debbie Delco

Debbie Agbottah, the eldest daughter, is soft spoken, her voice a whisper as she articulates respect and admiration for her mother. Utilizing a degree in public administration, Debbie began as an administrative assistant within the Education Service Center in Austin, Texas, assisting with the coordination of summer workshops and working with consultants on various projects. Then her sense of public duty led to a stint as admissions counselor for the University of Texas in Austin where she recruited potential college students and aided students and parents with admissions. From there she moved to a position as an administrator for the Section 8 Program and helped with the city of Terrell's federally assisted housing program. Then she returned to Austin to work for the Novishi Corporation as the assistant to the president before ultimately taking a job as a systems analyst IV for the Comptroller of Public Accounts in Austin. Throughout the years she has also been involved in arenas such as the Girl Scouts of America, school organizations, Jack & Jill of America, and The Links, Incorporated.

Loretta Edelen, the middle daughter, proved to be a vessel of contentment as she spoke to the harmony and allegiance her mother modeled. With degrees from Clark-Atlanta University and the University of Michigan, Loretta began work as an administrative intern for U.S. Congressman Wyche Fowler Jr., Fifth District of Georgia, in Washington, D.C. Then a return to Austin, Texas, led to three different career opportunities. First she served as a media intern for the Texas Employment Commission with primary projects focusing on career development materials for the state's high

Loretta Delco

Cheryl Delco

school students. Next she accepted a role as senior citizen coordinator, responsible for coordination of senior citizen voter registration and absentee voting during the Jake Pickle re-election campaign. And last, she moved to her current job as an institutional research manager for Austin Community College in Austin, Texas. Like Debbie, Loretta also has affiliations beyond the workplace. She has served as president of a local PTA, been appointed to advisory committees, and was elected and re-elected as a trustee for the Austin Independent School District.

Cheryl Sawyer, the youngest Delco daughter, is a take-charge woman, her composure a testament to the competency and self-reliance passed from mother to daughter. Cheryl's work background reveals fifteen years of diversified experience in persuasive, interpretive, and informative communication; development of innovative programs; and fund raising and strategic planning for public, nonprofit, and for-profit organizations. To carry out these roles, Cheryl has utilized a variety of venues: work as a Lyndon Baines Johnson congressional intern for U.S. Congressman George M. "Mickey" Leland in Washington, D.C., executive director for the Capitol Ballet Company of Washington, D.C., development associate for the American Red Cross National Headquarters, and director of corporate and foundation relations for KLRU-TV in Austin, Texas. Like her sisters, Cheryl is involved outside of work as a volunteer for the Black Arts Alliance and a community advisor for the City of Austin in different areas.

All in all, it seemed most fitting that the library had served as the spot where Debbie Agbottah, Loretta Edelen, and Cheryl Sawyer would speak about their mother, Wilhelmina Delco, as a positive role model in their lives.

Shia Shabazz Barnett

poet; author

Mother, Beverly Kilbourne; daughter, Shia Barnett;
granddaughter, Salihah

Beverly Antoinette Kilbourne

b. 1947

*Mother has always been my constant and my source of positivity, my source
for reinforcement about myself. With that for some time came pain, but now
I have a great respect and appreciation for our relationship. There's just
something that doesn't need to be said about the love we feel for each other.*

I REMEMBER I USED TO lay on Mom's lap when I was a kid and she would
stroke my face; she would just trace my face until I'd fall asleep. And I
remember she'd always comb out my hair. Then in 1990 she had an acci-
dent at work and became partially paralyzed in one arm. So this woman
who had always been active and had full use of both hands had to learn
to deal with what life sent her. I think about how it is so easy to take for
granted the things we do every day and especially the things we do with
our hands.

Of course, the use of your hands ties directly in with food and with cooking, but I guess I never ventured into how food and the events surrounding it connect us, how they bring people together. But what I have come to know is that a lot of lessons can be learned in the kitchen when you are cooking or gathered for a meal. Mother is a very good cook and has always been very thorough, almost perfect, in her preparations. But it is interesting in that there were some very heavy things happening in our family outside of the food and the meals, and I can see now that although every meal might be perfect, she was not.

What excites me now in coming back to food is that when I look at it, it has a symbolic basis for a lot of the things I learned as a result of the family matters I went through with my mother—things I learned about myself and about how to become who I am. So when I look at our relationship when we're in the kitchen, I think about how that is one place where we were and still are really mother and daughter. And the overwhelming emotion I associate with food and Mother is forgiveness.

Mom's food is well seasoned and so is she. She was the mother on the block that every kid loved, and she inspired such imagination and creativity in me. She really had such a way with theatrics that you just came to know everything about her was dramatic. She'd make up this pretend restaurant and I'd come to eat and she'd tell me all kinds of stories. She was a natural storyteller, and probably my favorite one was when I would be at the table and I'd get to be the princess and she'd sing to me, "Sheena, my little Sheena, she's so sweet, she's so doggone neat."

But her creative influence went further than the kitchen. She always had me in tap, ballet, jazz, art school, and tried to keep my imagination growing. We'd get dressed up and go to plays and she would inspire me about charm school and how important it was to be graceful. She just wanted me to be a well-rounded woman. I didn't understand all of that then, but now I see the importance of grace and the arts. And so I am thankful to her for trying to cultivate those things for me.

Going back to Mother, she has this child-like excitement, and even if it's in a little song she'll just stand up and sing it out. I remember one song she wrote that I loved was a little country song that kind of captures her. It went something like:

Well I put on a smile from a makeup case
because the years have given me a brand new face
and now I live in a world I don't even know,
but I know I can turn the clocks all back,
so I keep my youth in a memory sack

in case I want to reach inside and get away one day.
Well, ain't nothing 'bout yesterday that I don't love.
Bring back simple times and simple ways
like climbing trees and skinning knees
and children having fun,
and Lord, don't forget, penny bubble gum.

I think about that song and I understand her better. But I think about how there is a lot of noise that we think is music that actually takes us away from understanding our own voice. Well, my mother gave me my voice; she taught me how to sing. My first book, *My Soul Sings Acapella*, is deeply personal, and after she read it she called me and cried and I said, "Mama—are you OK? Are you OK?" But I think a part of what she was crying about was I had grown beyond the circumstances. I had learned a lot about myself and was on the way to becoming who I am. That was the first time we really dealt with some family issues.

She's always thoughtful and the first to reinforce my talents and spirit. Anytime I feel like I'm going through something, she gives me guidance based on the person she knows me to be. There has always been a flow to everything Mama does, and anytime I feel bad about how someone treats

Beverly Antoinette Kilbourne, 2000

me, she says, "People just don't know how to act around sensitive, kind people." She tells me I have a beautiful heart and it's okay to have a good heart. She has spent her love in the simplest of terms of our relationship trying to make sure I know that she loves me. I respect and honor her because she's my mother, and what I've come to know is that she's human. Now I am able to say that I don't fault her for anything.

> *. . . I want to be able to make sure my children's environment is positive and stimulating and loving and supportive, so really what I want to give them is what Mom gave me.*

Her legacy is one of perseverance and wisdom. She wants me to understand that I can do anything as long as I work hard at it. I think she experienced, in her youth, an injustice that traumatized her and she came back from that. She made some mistakes and she came back from those, then she came back from her paralysis. Now she says, "I'm going to do the best I can with what I have, and if I can accomplish things, Shia, think what you can achieve." Mom has found peace in herself, and that's what she wants to give me.

I don't think Mom understands how much she's given me despite everything that has happened. She's given me the ability and the desire to want to master myself and my talents and to want to give those things to the world. I believe we live in a society where everybody is struggling to some degree, but I want to be able to make sure my children's environment is positive and stimulating and loving and supportive, so really what I want to give them is what Mom gave me.

Mom is like a swan because swans glide smoothly and prettily, but I don't think they can fly. And Mom has raised me to fly while she just beautifully and charmingly swims.

One of my favorite dishes was Mom's chicken enchiladas. When she'd cook, her rhythm was just throwing things together and tasting everything. I remember oohing and aahing while she cooked.

Beverly's Chicken Enchiladas

Small corn tortillas
4 medium boneless, skinless chicken breasts
1 16-oz. can enchilada sauce
Colby/jack cheese, grated
1 small onion, chopped
Lettuce, lettuce
2 medium tomatoes, diced
Salt, pepper
1 8-oz. container sour cream (optional)

Clean and strip fat from chicken. In medium saucepan, boil chicken breasts. Lightly season water with salt as it comes to a boil. Boil until chicken is fully cooked (45-60 minutes on medium heat, covered). Drain, then shred chicken. Lightly season chicken to taste with salt and pepper.

In separate containers place shredded lettuce, grated cheese(s), and diced tomatoes.

Preheat oven to 375 degrees. Pour enchilada sauce into large skillet. Add ⅓ can water. Over medium heat, bring to light simmer. Place corn tortillas in sauce until softened. Remove tortillas; drain extra sauce back into skillet. Place softened tortillas onto flat baking pan. Sprinkle chicken, onion, and small amount of cheese into center of each tortilla. Roll tortilla and place overlapping fold down onto baking pan. Once pan is full, pour half of sauce over enchiladas. Sprinkle with cheese until covered. Pour remaining sauce; cover with foil. Bake 35-45 minutes. Garnish with lettuce, tomatoes, sour cream, and guacamole.

Bev's Guacamole

We used to taste the guacamole so much that it was almost gone before we could eat it with the enchiladas.

2 small/medium ripened avocados
Sour cream
Salt

Mash avocados together until creamy. Add sour cream and salt to taste.

Classic Root Beer Float

I can remember when Mom would say, "Let's go make some ice cream sodas," and it was like a celebration. My sister and I thought we must have done something really good.

Vanilla ice cream
1 can root beer soda

Scoop as much ice cream into a cup as possible. Pour root beer over ice cream until bubbles rise, nearly overflowing. Eat bubbles down and pour more soda over ice cream. Dig in!

Shia Shabazz Barnett

Shia Shabazz Barnett—just the melody of her name rolls around inside your head and when spoken floats into the air like musical notes swirling about the universe. And so it is understandable that Shia is by nature a maestro of words and images, a lyrical woman who looks inward for the life songs she sings.

And sing is what she does in her first book of poetry and prose, *My Soul Sings Acapella*. Her works reflect a cadence that caresses the reader with observations about people and life. In her prelude to the book she pens,

Tribal rhythms
Spiritual hymns
Slaves sing

Juke Joint stroll
Jazz and soul
Groove and swing

Street Corner tunes
Blues singers' croons
Smooth and mello

Funky be-bop
Rap and hip-hop

My soul sings a cappella.

Shia believes she must write about the life she has lived and experienced as a woman, as a black woman, as a daughter, as a wife, and as a mother.

Shia Shabazz Barnett
Photo courtesy of Fred Argir

Having tapped into her poetic voice, Shia is working on her second book, entitled *I Am: Turning Trials into Triumph*. And with that work she moves into the nonfiction genre. Driven by the knowledge that all people face challenges they have to deal with and that life is basically a struggle, Shia is compiling an illustrative collection of biographical narratives by people under the age of forty-five that capture diverse stories of those who have used adversity to become leaders, public speakers, and role models for their communities and the world.

Shia has gained wide recognition in coffeehouses and on university and college campuses across the country. She has been honored as a guest speaker and featured author at media events and literary engagements. She takes her passion for the arts further by facilitating poetry and creative writing workshops with young people. Other efforts resulted in her being the founder and director of "A Salute to African American Writers: A Celebration and Tea." Helping her to follow her bliss, Shia received a 1997-1998 Texas Commission on the Arts Literary Grant. She is working on a second collection of poetry titled *The Butterfly Woman*. And it seems quite symbolic that this beautiful woman whose spirit is metamorphosing her soul into words should be spreading her wings and, like a butterfly, soaring through the skies.

Diane Gonzales Bertrand

author; educator

Three generations: Consuelo Gonzales, Diane Bertrand,
Suzanne Bertrand, 1989

Consuelo Chauvin Gonzales

b. 1926

If I could freeze-frame an image, it would be of my mother bending over me.
I lie in bed feeling feverish and the back of her cool hand touches my cheek.
I remember her hand felt so good as I gained a comfort, a sense that I
wasn't alone in my illness because Mom was there.

OUR FAMILY IS CLOSE KNIT and that has a lot to do with my grand-mother, my mother's mother, who treasured family and who focused on the *familia*. The whole concept of *familia* is that you do because they're family, you do because you love them, you do because they would do the

25

Mother, Consuelo Gonzales, and daughter Diane, 1959

same for you. That concept is so important in the Mexican American household.

I would have to say that one of the best memories with my family is going to the beach at Port Aransas every year. My father said the first time I went I was three months old and I just sat in a picnic basket on the beach. Later I remember we fished, played in the water, and ate sand, you know, we did the whole bit. And those are the memories that mean the most to me because they brought us together as a family and it didn't cost much money. Many times we camped on the beach and would just be totally entertained. After all these years the beach is still a special family place.

Another special memory is that we didn't have a family dining room when I grew up, but my mother had a kitchen with a big table my father built out of ornamental iron and that's where everything happened. When she cooked we were underfoot. We did homework there, we played with our toys there, and when my father would get an idea about something to build, he'd grab a pencil and start drawing on the Formica top. I mean everything happened in my mother's kitchen.

Another thing about our family was we went to church every Sunday. My father tells this wonderful story about the first week after they got married. It had snowed one of the rare Texas snows, and my mother had gotten up and was getting dressed. He asked her where she was going and she said, "I go to church every Sunday, Gilbert, and I'm going today as well," so he decided he'd better go with her. She was so committed that he became just as faithful a churchgoer as she was, and my mother saw to it that we went to church no matter where we were. Why even on our vacations we'd get up on a Sunday at 6:30 in the morning and try and find an eight o'clock mass somewhere. Of course we'd almost always get lost and sometimes were so late we'd have to sit in the car and wait for the 9:30 mass.

Mother made me feel like I was the most important child to her, and yet I have six siblings who would say the exact same thing. She made us feel special by making time for each of us. I had a defining moment about how my mother was connected to all of us kids when after my second child I realized that these two kids were mine for the rest of my life. And I remember thinking that my parents had seven ways to say I love you to me and all my siblings, and that is when I realized I could have my mother as a friend, as a fellow woman who had also had children. After that I started sitting with her more often at the table, baby in hand, nursing a baby, and just talking to her about things I was feeling. And it's because of her example that I try and make time for each of my children as individuals, that I don't choose one over the other.

Through all her examples, there has been one strong quality I associate with Mother—resilience. There's a flexibility in Mother. She is one of the most "make the best of what you have" people I know. I have no recollections of her complaining about a lack of money, wearing hand-me-over

Fiftieth wedding anniversary for Consuelo and Gilbert Gonzales, daughters Chris MacRae and Diane Bertrand, February 1989

Diane Bertrand and mother, Consuelo Gonzales

clothes, or living on the beach for a week as part of a family vacation. She took what she was given and did what she could to make it work.

Even now as she has struggled with a variety of health problems, she makes the best of it no matter what she gets tossed. She continues to make do even though her vision is weakening and she has had to learn how to write with her left hand and she must turn her head to compensate for deafness in one ear. I know that some days it's hard for her to accept her physical limitations, but she doesn't let them get her down. She still has a wonderful sense of humor and isn't bitter. I admire her persistence and I learn valuable lessons about dignity, faith, and love every time I'm with her.

But one thing I think was hardest for me and my sister was the time we had the job of feeding Mother after her surgery. When she was partially paralyzed and could not feed herself, we had to take on that role for her and it tapped into strengths that neither one of us ever thought we had. That was difficult because we had to take on a new role, but I think it made us recognize what a woman will do for her mother or for another woman. The emotion I would put with that was earthshaking. It shook me from my head to my toes to have to be that for my mother.

Mom showed me how to raise children, how to be a good Christian, and how to be a woman who could do a lot of things. I can be a writer, a teacher, a mother, a wife, and everything else because I saw the way she juggled things.

Consuelo's Sopa de Fideo

Mother's fideo is a favorite food. It's inexpensive, so I imagine we ate a lot of it for that reason. My biggest memory was trying to keep the noodles on a fork or spoon from the plate to my mouth.

> I box vermicelli noodles (about 8 oz.)

Coat bottom of frying pan with oil (about I tablespoon). Brown vermicelli in skillet and stir while browning. When vermicelli is brown, add:

> ½ small onion, chopped
> I clove garlic, minced or mashed
> ½ tsp. cumin powder
> ¼ bell pepper, chopped
> I medium tomato, chopped
> I tsp. salt (to taste)

Cover mixture with hot water (about 4 cups). Bring to boil, cover pot, simmer until done (about 15 minutes). Stir occasionally; add water if needed.

Note: The vermicelli is almost dry when cooked, so more water may be added to keep mixture like a soup. Chicken broth can also be added for flavoring.

Consuelo's Salsa de Chile

(hot sauce in a *molcajete*)

This recipe is about artistry. I was fascinated watching Mother char the tomato until the skin got burned, popped open, and the pulpy insides spurted out. I'd watch her peel the tomato on a plate then she'd get the molcajete. Using the rock, she'd mash the tomato into a thick sauce then chop up peppers and onions and stir them into the tomato mush. This artistic endeavor usually occurred on Sunday morning after church.

> I large tomato
> 1-3 hot peppers (serrano, piquin, etc.), cut into small pieces
> ½ small onion, minced

Char skin of tomato over stove burner or place in hot water until skin pops and is removable. Mash skinned tomato in *molcajete*. Add cut up peppers and onion to *molcajete*. Salt and pepper to taste.

Spoon mixture over scrambled eggs, a bowl of *caldo*, rice, or beans; eat it on a hot corn tortilla; or scoop and eat with fried tortilla chips. This chile can also be prepared with a food processor, but you miss the sting of the chile in the air. If you add 3 smashed avocados, you have a terrific guacamole. (Add a little lemon juice to keep guacamole from turning dark.)

Consuelo's Calabacita

Before I put this recipe in the book I had to test it out (since Mom never "measured"). Imagine my excitement when the calabacita tasted just as good as my mother's. And now I have the recipe!

I lb. lean pork steak, cut in small pieces
   (cut up chicken parts may be used in place of pork)
I ½ c. water (enough to cover meat)
I tsp. salt
½ tsp. black pepper
I garlic clove, minced or mashed
I tsp. powdered cumin
½ bell pepper, chopped
I small onion, chopped
2 medium tomatoes, chopped
3 Mexican squash or zucchini, cubed
2 ears fresh corn or I can whole kernel corn, drained

Cook meat in water with all seasonings and bell pepper, onion, and tomatoes for 20 minutes over medium flame. Stir occasionally until all flavors combine. Meanwhile, cut up squash in small cubes and add them to pot. Cover and simmer 20 minutes more, stirring occasionally. Finally add fresh corn from cob or can. Cook another 10 minutes. Season with more salt to liking. After cooking, turn off flame and let pot stand for 10 minutes. Serve in bowls.

Diane Theresa Gonzales Bertrand

When you walk into Diane Gonzales Bertrand's home, you immediately know that a belief and pride in *la familia* lies at the core of the household. Sprinkled throughout rooms are pictures that invite a sense of comfort and freeze-frame generations of her extended families. And central to it all is the large table, a gathering spot that serves as the hub at which much of the daily life occurs. Immediately after the interview began, it was *la familia* that became the focus of Diane's memories, words, and praises.

Diane Gonzales Bertrand

And that family extends to her relatives and to the Mexican American culture, a culture about which she writes and celebrates through her words as a writer of young adult fiction and poetry.

Diane credits her writer's sense to a love of reading that was formed out of necessity in a family of seven children where her parents found the least expensive form of entertainment to be trips to the local library. Diane, who loved to conjure up make-believe playmates as a child, eventually transferred that creative imagination to the written page. Even as a fifth grader, Diane's course seemed set when she began a story about a boyfriend and girlfriend—based on two real-life friends. She continued the story over a course of eight or nine years, eventually filling more than seventy-five notebooks. And so it was that Diane's dedicated writing muse called her to pen tales.

To date Diane's list of published works includes: *Trino's Choice*; *Lessons of the Game*; *Sip, Slurp, Soup, Soup—Caldo, Caldo, Caldo*; *Alicia's Treasure*, and *Sweet Fifteen*, all published by Houston-based Arte Público Press. Three more works, *Carousel of Dreams*, *Close to the Heart*, and *Touchdown for Love*, have been published by Avalon Books. Diane also has had poetry published in *Palo Alto Review*, *Concho River Review*, *English in Texas*, and *Chile Verde Review*.

Her professional career as a published author followed another in education. In 1979 Diane began teaching at two San Antonio schools in the same neighborhood where she was reared. Then in 1983 she joined the faculty of Holy Cross High School, remaining there until 1988 when she left teaching to stay home with her two young children. After attending graduate school, Diane began working at St. Mary's University and from there she pursued writing seriously.

Diane credits her parents for her confidence in believing she can do anything she wants if she works hard. As an adult Diane often turns to her mother for advice when frustrations get in the way. And based on her mother's advice—not to compromise values or traditions—Diane keeps her focus on what she wishes to accomplish. So it is natural that this daughter, wife, mother, and sibling often turns to her roots and to her lifetime rich in *familia* as she lays foundations for works that capture aspects of the Mexican American culture.

Eleanor Marie Totty Bonner and daughter, Cathy Bonner, 1999

Eleanor Marie Totty Bonner

b. 1928

I think of my mother as Rosie the Riveter. She was the kind of woman who got in there and worked a job that wasn't always a glamour job. She always worked hard to earn half the family income while keeping the home fires burning at the same time.

MY MOTHER MARRIED MY FATHER shortly before he left the States during WW II, and to help out, her father, who had worked for the railroad, got her into telegraph school out in Hollywood, California. So at eighteen years old she was living in another state by herself and earning a living while her husband was in the Army.

My mother's a strong individual who thinks of men's and women's roles very traditionally, yet she's always worked and that was unique. In the 1950s when everybody else's mom stayed at home to bake cookies and be there when the kids got home from school, she worked. She worked hard and one of the traits I got from her was being willing to work hard. From her I also learned to be responsible and think for myself and not rely on someone else to solve my problems. Her working I guess made us more independent than our peers because we all had chores and were expected to help keep the house straight. We were just expected to fend for ourselves.

One time I remember telling her I felt sorry for her because she had to work, but she said, "Sorry for me? I love working." She liked getting out of the house and making her own money and not having to ask Daddy for it, and she liked being able to spend the money she earned exactly as she wanted. So that was her preference, but I never knew that and thought it was a burden to have to work and raise a family.

By watching Mother, all of us kids got the idea you were supposed to work, so we started jobs at about fourteen years old and that helped us grow up faster. When I think about it, I preferred that Mother worked because she was a mom who wouldn't let us sit around and be idle. I remember when I was twelve or thirteen I wanted to be a lawyer. I'd take the bus downtown to the courthouse and sit in trials to watch the lawyers and judges then I would go visit Mother at her job before I'd go back home.

After work she'd come home though and not do anything else but take care of us kids. She didn't go off and have drinks after work; instead she did laundry every night and took us places on the weekends. I remember when I was small she would let me have slumber parties and we'd sleep outside in a tent or on cots. When she had extra time she was great about birthday parties and doing special things for us, but Mother didn't hover over us. She had been an only child with a protective mother who pushed her into a lot of activities and lessons, so Mother didn't want us to feel like we had to do something just because she wanted it. Since she had felt smothered, she vowed to be independent and let her children grow up independently. And we all did.

And that attitude carried over to the philosophy my mother had about education, that it was important to make good grades and learn the basics. As long as we were getting that, she wasn't really worried. I don't remember her ever intervening because she didn't have time to be involved, and I don't remember her going to school except maybe once a year on Parent's Night. Again, I think that gave me a streak of independence to realize I was responsible for myself. It made me stand on my own two feet because there wasn't going to be any parent rescuing me and saying to a teacher, "You're not going to treat my child like that." It was always understood that I was to get in there, do what the teacher said, and fight my own battles.

My mother is street smart and has good core values of resourcefulness, honesty, and kindness. Everything she knows she basically taught herself, and that makes her unique because she can figure out how to get something done. It seems like other mothers were always waiting for their husbands to get home to fix something, but that was never the case with Mother. She could fix a tire and the plumbing or put on a wedding reception. She would just figure out how to get things done and she'd do them, and I think I learned from her how to get things done.

> *My mother is street smart and has good core values of resourcefulness, honesty, and kindness. Everything she knows she basically taught herself, and that makes her unique because she can figure out how to get something done.*

Mother also believes in doing the right thing and being kind. She would never cheat anybody out of anything. She's the type that if you gave her too much change she'd give it back to you. I remember once when I was little I took a candy dispenser from a store. She figured out what I had done, so she made me go back and give the owner money. I was totally humiliated but it certainly taught me a lesson about being honest. I think she feels like she provided us with the basics and that since we had a very safe, loving home her kids could soar on their own.

And she's so kind and generous. She's always willing to help people who need it and who are not as well off as our family. I remember one time she worked with a Cuban refugee who basically just had the clothes on his back. She not only helped him get clothes but she also helped his fianceé come here and then she put on their wedding. And that's just like Mother, trying to help somebody. She's always had lots of friends who gravitate toward her because she is considerate and will remember things that are important to them.

Mother doesn't complain now and she surely didn't when we were children. I remember she'd always give me this piece of advice, "Life's not fair, get over it and quit whining." Like I can remember when I first started driving I locked my purse in the car when I went into a store; when I came back out the window had been broken and my purse stolen. I was so upset—because at fourteen you think life has come to an end when you lose your billfold—but she just told me to get over it because things like that were going to happen. See, with Mother there's no feeling sorry for yourself, and I think that is a valuable lesson because it's so realistic.

Once she retired, my mother and father had a farm for many years, so she was always out on the tractor plowing up the garden and planting something. She had a huge garden, more than she could ever need, so she was always giving things to her neighbors. And I can still see her wearing the straw hat and sitting on that tractor while my father sat on the front porch and watched her. Her health has gotten a little worse now and they have sold the farm, but I know she would like to be digging in the dirt again. I know she misses that garden.

Mother's greatest gift is not anything tangible. No, it would be the ability to see something that needs to be planned, executed, and completed. She would never be one in a crisis to stand around wringing her hands, so I guess her gift is giving me the ability to accomplish something from conception to task.

Cobbler

Two piecrusts
2 c. berries
1½ c. sugar
5 tsp. flour
¼ tsp. cinnamon
Dabs of butter
¼ c. water

Mix together and pour into the piecrust. Place second crust on top and sprinkle with sugar. Bake for 30 to 40 minutes at 350 degrees.

Creamy Orange Fluff

2 pkg. (3 oz.) orange gelatin
2½ c. boiling water
2 cans (11 oz. each) mandarin oranges, drained
1 can (8 oz.) crushed pineapple, undrained

1 can (6 oz.) frozen orange juice concentrate, thawed

Topping:

1 pkg. (8 oz.) cream cheese, softened
1 c. cold milk
1 pkg. (3.4 oz.) instant vanilla pudding mix

In a bowl, dissolve gelatin in boiling water. Stir in oranges, pineapple, and orange juice concentrate. Coat a 13 x 9 x 2 inch dish with nonstick cooking spray; add gelatin mixture. Refrigerate until firm. In a mixing bowl, beat cream cheese until light. Gradually add milk and pudding mix. Beat until smooth. Spread over orange layer. Chill until firm. Yield: 12-16 servings.

Cathy Bonner

The not too distant sounds of cars whizzing by on a nearby thoroughfare provided a backdrop as I sat on Cathy Bonner's front porch. Having arrived early, I opted for the open air rather than the car's stuffiness as I waited, but before long Cathy drove up and welcomed me into her home. As I sat on her couch waiting for her, I noted the order and elegance among the furnishings and figured Ms. Bonner to be a woman who lives with a keen sense of certainty. My musings turned out to be on the mark.

To borrow the title of "Rosie the Riveter" that Cathy ascribed to her mother, I concluded about midway through the interview that it also described Cathy Bonner. She is an independent woman, a pragmatic woman, whose certitude evokes a nuts-and-bolts approach to achievement. Working from a prudent belief about proficiency, she

Cathy Bonner

delivers work as a builder, a blueprint maker, who—to paraphrase her words—asserts that most of her life's work has started out in dreams that have become realities.

As a 1972 graduate of the University of Texas in Austin, she was recognized with the Outstanding Student Award and with selection as a Student Senator. From there she started paving her road to career successes. In 1974 she created Bonner Incorporated, a marketing consulting firm specializing in strategic planning, advertising, public relations, and direct response campaigns. She successfully recruited a QVC Telemarketing Service Center and twenty Venture Stores and distribution centers to Texas, obtained loan and export trade support for businesses resulting in the commitment of more than six billion dollars in private investment capital, and helped increase tourism in Texas. She also specialized in marketing state-sponsored tuition-saving programs.

Working as executive director for the Texas Department of Commerce from 1991 to 1994, Cathy was instrumental in the passing of legislation to create the Texas Smart Jobs Fund that finances the creation of new jobs by funding customized training programs. Also for three consecutive years her efforts proved fruitful in helping to create more jobs within Texas than any other state. She accepted a gubernatorial appointment to lead Texas's economic development, international trade, tourism, and workforce training agency, and during that time she managed a staff of over four hundred professionals and a biennial budget of over five million dollars.

However, shouldering a belief in hard work, Cathy Bonner's efforts encompass other arenas. She has served as president of the board of the Foundation for Women's Resources for more than twenty-five years and is founder of its current project, The Women's Museum: An Institute for the Future (Dallas). It is her dream that this place will honor past accomplishments of American women and shape the future for generations to come. She also founded Leadership Texas and Leadership America, has served as chairperson for the Mayor's Mobility Task Force, and is an ongoing board member for the Lone Star Girl Scout Council.

Cathy Bonner says that from her mother she learned the value of working hard, fending for herself, standing on her own two feet, and doing the right thing, so it is without question that this mother's lessons live through her daughter's contributions.

Anne Garrett McDermett

b. 1889

I think a real good word for Mama is dreamer; she was a dreamer with a foundation under her yet she had visions of sugarplums.

Anne Garrett McDermett

MAMA WAS THE PERFECT HOMEMAKER and mother. She sewed pretty well, and even though she didn't like to sew she made everything I wore. But I remember how she just labored over these things, and I remember she'd wake me up in the middle of the night and say, "Get up and try this on, I think I've figured out what I need to do." You see, Mama never wanted to go exactly by the pattern because she said that didn't have any spirit, and those clothes were labors of love. And Mama was a great one for making do. She made over lots of stuff for me to wear because you see we'd get hand-me-downs from one of her sisters and she'd cut them up and make them over for me. My auntie would send a coat, and Mama could get a little suit out of it. You just never felt bad about what you didn't have because Mama would just make do.

And she was a good cook. I especially loved the chocolate cake she made and, oh, one thing I remember, I could always tell when it was fall because I'd get off the school bus and as I got close to the house I could smell soup. You know Mama cooked kind of like she sewed, so she'd add to and cut around. Now I guess she had a basic recipe, but then she added all this other stuff herself. She was pretty creative.

Living on our ranch was a great independence for me. I had nobody to play with so I fooled around with Mama and Daddy or I rode this horse and imagined I was anybody I wanted to be. But then everything I did in Cross Plains Mama knew about it by the time I got home. I guess that's because my dad and Mr. Fred, who lived on the next ranch, had set up their own telephone poles and hooked up to the central office. So when the phone rang, everybody on our road who was tied into that line picked up and we just knew everybody else's business.

Well one Sunday I had ridden on the back of a motorcycle in town, and when Mama found out about it she was livid. She had just given me hell about doing that when my aunt came up and started talking about what I'd done. I was in the other room and I heard Mama defending me to the nth degree, so when my aunt left I said to Mama, "Why did you just give me hell about this then defend me to your sister?" She put her arm around me and said, "Toody, you need to remember this about your mother, every crow thinks hers is the blackest."

Now Mama taught me about the belief in the ultimate goodness of man. I think that was a built-in philosophy of hers about caring not just for us but for other people as well. I remember she'd often say, "There is something good in the worst of us, and something bad in the best of us, so it hardly behooves any of us to talk about the rest of us." That was Mama. She just didn't let us talk about people.

And she was a good hostess. I remember when thirty or forty men would come to help with the wheat threshing and would stop to eat lunch, well Mama would insist we'd have iced tea, cobbler, and cloth napkins. Can you believe it, cloth napkins. Why, one time after I married, Mama had a stroke and we were all up there because we thought she was going to die. I remember she motioned for me to come over, and I thought she was going to give me some last words, but she said, "Toody, make coffee, there's cake in the crystal cake plate. Serve all these people who are here because we have to have refreshments for them." I couldn't believe it, but it was important to her that these people at our house be comfortable. She was just charming, no matter what.

Another thing, Mama was always saying verses, and after she said a verse two or three times you were supposed to know it. And she always told me to never stop in the middle of a verse because nobody wants to hear half of anything. So we'd do this for hours, usually while she ironed. Mama had this little stool and when we'd have guests she'd feed them coffee and cake then she'd get this stool and say, "Do you want to hear the baby say a little verse?" Now imagine, I'm three or four years old and I'd always say the same little verse, "Roses on my shoulders, slippers on my feet, I'm my daddy's baby, don't you think I'm sweet?" This was a big deal with Mama, and I guess whoever came to visit had to hear the baby say a little verse.

> *. . . a built-in philosophy of hers about caring not just for us but for other people as well. I remember she'd often say, "There is something good in the worst of us, and something bad in the best of us, so it hardly behooves any of us to talk about the rest of us."*

I never knew anybody who wanted to go to college more than Mama—she really was the original lifetime learner—but after the big war, the Civil War, her mother said the family was impoverished so she couldn't go. But I still think of Mama as a learner. She'd put me down for my nap and every time I woke up she was reading. She never worked in the fields or outside much because she didn't like to get messed up, but she loved having this time to herself. She'd sit in the big front room over by the windows that looked out onto the farmland, and that's where she'd read most of the time. And she always had a book in the kitchen, so when she'd put things on to cook then she'd read. She always said to me, "An unused mind grows stagnant."

When I close my eyes I can feel Mama holding my face. She'd talk to me a lot by holding my face, and sometimes she patted it. I can see her helping me with my homework, and I can see her hands writing letters and making notes. Mama had beautiful hands and took care of her skin. She wore white cotton gloves and used Golden Peacock Bleach Cream all the time. You know I think her hands looked better when she died than mine did at twenty.

Mama had been in a nursing home when my sister called to say the doctor gave her forty-five minutes to live. It was about five hours before I got to the home, and when I did my sister said, "Toody, I think she's waiting for you. She's fought for every breath since I called you." When I walked over to her I said, "Mama," and she just stopped twisting in the bed and opened her eyes and smiled. Now I don't handle those things well, so I caught hold of her hand and she squeezed mine.

I said, "Mama, this is not small talk. I want to talk to you about how much I appreciate you making my prom dress. I know you spent hours because it had to look just like Miss Scarlett's, and I remember you got me up in the middle of the night four nights in a row to try it on. But it was a labor of love and I knew that." Then I said, "Mama, I want to tell you how much it meant for you to teach me your little verses."

I was just talking to her, and if anybody had told me I could sit there by my mother and watch her die, I would have said they're crazy. But I just talked to her, and she was holding my hand and her breath just got shorter and shorter. I said, "Mama, I guess you're the smartest woman I've ever known, and I don't think I told you near enough what a difference you made in my life and how much I loved you."

She was just holding my hand and suddenly she wasn't. You know, it was a closure, and I do think she was aware.

My two favorite pieces of advice from Mama were, "Remember honey, you can get a lot of things done if you don't care who gets the credit," and "Don't make small talk, Toody, you're just talking to hear your brains rattle."

During most of my life Mama cooked on a wood-burning stove, so she watched and guessed at the time it took for her cookies to be done. As I recall, she knew exactly how many pages of her book she could read before she took the cookies from the oven. Fifteen minutes at 350 degrees works for me. These cookies and a glass of milk were my treat when I got up from my nap and later as my snack when I came home from school.

Old-Fashioned Tea Cakes

1 c. butter
3 eggs
1 tsp. baking powder
Pinch of salt
2 c. sugar
4 c. flour
1 tsp. vanilla flavoring (lemon flavoring can be used, but Daddy didn't like lemon)

Mix together and make a roll. Roll out with rolling pin on floured bread board until dough is thin. Cut with biscuit cutter, sprinkle top with sugar, place on a greased and floured cookie sheet, and bake until light brown.

Date Loaf Candy

3 c. sugar
½ c. water
½ c. Carnation milk
Pinch of salt
1 c. dates, chopped
2 Tbsp. butter
1 c. pecans, chopped

Mix together sugar, water, milk, and salt in saucepan and boil until sugar dissolves. Add dates, stirring constantly until a soft ball can be formed. Add butter and beat until creamy then add nuts. Pour out on a cold wet cloth and knead until a smooth, long roll is formed. Cool and cut as needed. It is better to cut off only what is being served and keep the rest rolled up and in a cool place.

Curried Fruit

 1 can sliced peaches
 1 can sliced pears
 1 can apricots
 1 can chunk pineapple
 1 can mandarin oranges

Drain all fruit, mix, and place in long, shallow baking dish. Sprinkle ½ cup brown sugar and 1 tablespoon of curry powder over fruit, then dot with ½ cup of butter. Cook one hour. At the end of 45 minutes add maraschino cherries and ½ cup of pecans. Serve hot . . . . great with ham!

Toody Byrd

The world is a warmer place, a better place because of women like Toody Byrd. Yet how do you capture this pint-sized lady in words since the list of all she encompasses would be endless. As Toody travels about the country speaking to groups, she attributes her foundation for believing in the ultimate goodness of man to her mama, and today her mama would be proud to know the role she modeled for her daughter has taken root.

Toody is like a robin, a harbinger of high spirits and hopes for goodwill to anyone within one hundred yards of her. A soprano-like voice is her hallmark, a hallmark that once it takes up residence in a person's psyche stays there forever, waiting to resurface whenever summoned. In this role, Toody is a maternal guardian of accord, fairness, and unconditional love, and the lives she has touched are countless.

She often talks about how her mama used to say to her, "Don't make small talk, Toody, you're just talking to hear your brains rattle," so Toody took that advice to heart. Each and every day of her lifetime she avoids small talk and makes certain her words have meaning. To get those words out to as many souls as possible, Toody taps into her boundless energy to offer her laughter and joy, her insight and wisdom.

How fitting then that Toody Byrd has spent a lifetime dealing with people. After receiving undergraduate and graduate degrees, Toody taught English, social studies, and various other subjects all over Texas. Her next step was in the role of a school counselor. And in that position, she accrued a long list of recognitions: American School Counselors' Writing Award, Outstanding Counselor of Texas Award, Nominee for the 1984 Texas

Toody Byrd

Women's Hall of Fame, Ninth Recipient of the Key Communicator Award, and the 1989 Presidential Award from the Texas Association of Counseling and Development. But perhaps the recognition that encapsulates Toody most accurately was being declared a State Treasure by the 71st Legislature of the State of Texas.

She is truly a treasure who has served as a consultant in areas that include teaching migrant students, peer pressure, parenting, divorce, motivation, self-image, aging, sex education, and HIV.

In 1991 she retired as director of guidance and student services for the Eanes Independent School District in Austin, Texas, and began traveling as a motivational speaker and workshop leader. Those travels have taken her to thirty-five states as the keynote speaker at state conferences. In 1998 she added the title of author to her résumé when she wrote *Toody Byrd Talks and Talks and Talks, etc.*, a book of wit and wisdom.

So you see, Toody did listen to her mama about not making small talk. To borrow a cliché, Toody definitely walks the walk and talks the talk, and in her case, Toody Byrd's words represent the woman behind them.

Liz Carpenter

former press secretary, Lady Bird Johnson; author

Mary Elizabeth Robertson Sutherland

b. 1887

Mother knew who she was and she knew our roots were strengthened by the pioneer types that came to Texas. She knew that she wanted her children to have a college education and that the core of life was faith and love.

WHEN I THINK OF MY MOTHER I think of a comfortably plump, huggable woman with a shoulder to lean on. She was a soft-spoken woman and I never heard her raise her voice and never heard her yell at anybody. She was the ultimate in calmness and had an unshakable steadiness. I always knew she would be there every afternoon when I came into the house after school, and I knew I could always tell her what happened that day.

I think of her as being full of stories and the center for all of us, my brothers, sisters, and even my cousins. She always had a lap that accommodated two children, and when we were little kids we'd gather around and she'd tell us her polecat stories from when she lived on the ranch. Mother had this gift of words, and she was somebody whose words counted. She was a wordsmith and a reader who grew up studying years of Latin in this little town of Salado, Texas. Later she studied at what is now known as Texas Woman's University.

Our roots were deep in Texas because both my grandmother and grandfather had arrived in the 1830s and were a part of history. But

Mary Elizabeth
Robertson Sutherland

47

one of the things I think about is that there really was a common thread that ran through so many of the women on these lonely ranches in the rural south. They knew the British poets. My mother would quote poetry from these poets, and it could have been in the bedroom, in the kitchen, along with a conversation, or whenever the occasion arose, and I can still remember those phrases she quoted all the time. I guess these women could escape the dishpan better if they quoted poetry over it. So while their husbands were out branding or doctoring cattle, these ladies had something that fed their souls.

As I said, Mother had a poem for everything, and it was a wonderful, rich inheritance that marks my life. We just lived with words and poetry so I have a heritage of words that were spoken in our home; I've earned my living with words, as a reporter, a journalist, an author, and a public speaker and it all springs from her. But Mother was also a reader. I remember she'd get everything cleaned up early on Thursdays because that was the day she got the *Saturday Evening Post*. Her dream was to crawl up in bed, have an apple, and read without getting interrupted. She cherished that time.

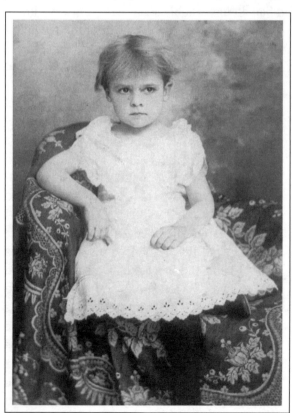

Young Mary Elizabeth Robertson Sutherland

I'm lucky I have a family who saves letters. I remember that she and my grandmother would sit by this trunk of letters from our ancestors and read them aloud. Here they were reading these letters and being enthralled by the Texas history their ancestors had been part of. Mother gave me such a love of those who have gone before that she shaped my career without knowing she was doing it. We were just immersed in that history, and I'm so glad because it gives you such confidence to know who's gone before.

We never had money, I mean we were really short, but we never felt poor. We felt rich with family tales and rich that we had a place to belong, and she wanted us to be proud of our roots. Another thing, Mother always had faith in God and told us to have faith in ourselves, and I know she had such faith in us. I mean, my brother George and I would get on a horse, ride down to the center of town, go under the Stagecoach Inn, and play in a cave. My gosh, there could have been rattlesnakes or moccasins, but I don't think she worried much.

You know I think space gives a sense of humor to a lot of Texas people because of the blue skies and fleecy white clouds, and Mother had a good sense of humor. I remember her saying to us often, "See the humor of the situation," and there's a funny story that goes with that. She was busy one day and my younger brother George had a BB gun and he told Mama to hold up her hand. Well, she held up her hand and he shot her. Of course everybody felt terrible, but this little kid with a BB gun wanted a target, and she gave it to him, and she just stood there and roared, laughing at herself.

If I close my eyes, I can still see Mother putting her hands in the biscuit dough and kneading it, then putting it on a floured bread board, rolling it out and gently cutting biscuits with the top of a fruit jar or a glass, and finally putting them in the oven. I can see her hands at the sewing machine making a pink tulle evening gown for me when I was in high school, and it seemed like the tulle just went for miles and miles. I remember that.

She always said to remember who you are and make something of yourself, and those words still come back to me a lot. When she died I was in Washington, D.C., and I wish I had come home and spent some time with her, but I was pregnant with my second child. Her death was very much a surprise, and I wish I had been there for it. You know you look back and regret how many times you didn't say "I love you" to your mother. It's just never enough.

I can find no fault in Mama and I miss her a lot, and there's regret on my part that I didn't make more of the time she was here. I would give anything if I could have had more time with her. And if I could thank her for anything, it would be for just loving me and giving love, for hugging me and making me feel very secure.

I believe the quotation on Mother's tombstone captures what she meant to all of us; it reads, "She was the best evidence of an Almighty loving spirit for nothing else could have created her."

Mary Elizabeth
Robertson Sutherland

The following recipes were taken from the handwritten recipe book put together by Mary Elizabeth Robertson Sutherland for Alice Sutherland Romberg. Recipes have remained as written to preserve their authenticity. The title page reads, "The very best wishes for happiness to Alice and John Romberg. September 3, 1939."

Spoon Bread

Sift ½ teaspoon salt and ⅓ cup of corn meal into 4 cups of sweet milk and stir over slow fire until it thickens. Remove from fire and stir into the mixture 4 well beaten eggs. Beat mixture well and pour into boiling dish. Sit dish in pan with a little hot water in it and boil on medium heat until it is of custard like consistency and brown on top. This is a recipe from the Priscilla cookbook that I have used a long while.

Devil's Food Cake by Aunt Gladys

2 c. sifted flour
1 tsp. soda
½ c. butter
1¼ c. brown sugar
2 eggs
3 sq. melted Baker's unsweetened chocolate
1 c. milk
1 tsp. vanilla

Sift flour and soda together three times. Cream butter and sugar. Add one egg at a time beating well after each. Add chocolate. Blend. Add flour alternately with one cup milk, beating well. Add vanilla. Bake in two greased, deep layer pans. Moderate oven - 30 minutes. Use chocolate filling.

Minute Fudge Frosting by Lucile Robertson

¼ c. butter or margarine
½ c. cocoa
¼ c. milk
1 c. sugar
⅛ tsp. salt

Melt the butter. Add rest of ingredients, stirring over low heat until sugar is dissolved. Bring to a full rolling boil and boil 1 minute. Remove from heat and beat immediately until creamy enough to spread. I use it all the time. Quick, easy and good. L.

Date Roll by Lois H. Sutherland

3 c. sugar
1 c. milk
1 lb. dates (cut)
1 c. pecans
Vanilla

Cook all until thick, beat until stiff then roll in damp cloth. Put in icebox until cold. Cut in thin slices.

White Cake

Whites of 8 eggs, beaten well and added last
2 c. sugar
1 c. butter
1 c. sweet milk
3 c. flour, which has been sifted about five times and then had 2 rounded teaspoons of baking powder added to it.
1 tsp. vanilla

Cream the butter, then add the sugar slowly, add the milk and flour alternately and the whites of eggs last. If you use a butter substitute, don't put quite a cupful in. You can use the same recipe for gold cake, only using the egg yolks beaten till light. I always put waxed paper, bread paper will do, greased in the bottom of the cake pan. Cook in very moderate oven with a pan of water in the bottom of the oven. After the cake is firm, if it needs to brown a little, take the water out. You can make a pink and white or marble cake by dividing the cake batter and adding either fruit coloring or chocolate to one pan of batter and dropping it in alternate spoonfuls in the pan with the white.

This makes a large cake; you can make a fair sized one by cutting the recipe in half. It is called white cake, silver cake, and bride's cake.

Liz Carpenter

On the visit to the home of Liz Carpenter, a sense of serenity embraced me as I steadily climbed the road that wiggled through the woods and ended at a leveling-off place where Liz' rambling, one-story house stood. Its front facade consisting primarily of plate glass windows invited a panoramic view of the hills below and of downtown Austin. The entire setting seemed ideal for a woman whose roles in life have been so vastly encompassing.

As we ate lunch in the dining room, Liz spoke of her marriage in 1944 to Leslie Carpenter and then the births of their two children, Scott and Christy. She talked about one of life's little surprises when the family grew to include her brother's three children for whom she became a surrogate mother.

She then talked about her involvement in politics and communications. After securing a journalism degree from the University of Texas in Austin, she went to Washington, D.C. in 1942 and covered presidents from FDR to LBJ. It was when Lyndon Baines Johnson was nominated as vice president in 1960 that Liz was invited to join him. She accepted and that led to her serving as the first woman executive assistant to a vice president until 1963 when President John F. Kennedy was assassinated. After that Liz served as press secretary and staff director to Lady Bird Johnson.

The joyful glint in her eyes as she recalled those days gave way to infectious laughter as she then talked about her involvement in women's groups and issues. Liz talked about jumping aboard the ERA ratification trail as one of the founders of the National Women's Political Caucus in 1971. Then with pride she listed other opportunities that included being tapped by President Ford for the International Women's Year commission in both 1976 and 1980, serving under President Carter as the assistant secretary of education for public affairs, and serving as president of the Women's National Press Club. And so it only seems natural that she was inducted into the Texas Women's Hall of Fame by former Governor Mark White.

Liz spoke of her place in the world of communications and the honor of having the College of Liberal Arts at the University of Texas establish the Liz Sutherland Carpenter Distinguished Lectureship to serve as an arena for prominent speakers. And last, Liz spoke about her latest involvement as an advocate for aging Americans. And so it is that this woman whose family roots grow deep stands as a model of dedication to living life to its fullest. But perhaps Erma Bombeck said it best when she said about Liz Carpenter that "no one remains the same person after meeting [her]."

Mary Elizabeth "Liz" Sutherland Carpenter
Photo by Jim Dougherty, Photographer

Vivian Castleberry
former women's editor, *Dallas Times Herald*; author

Jessie Lee Henderson Anderson

b. 1896

Mother was a spiritual person without being overtly religious. She was just devoutly, deeply spiritual and had this old Presbyterian feeling that everything was going to turn out all right.

MOTHER WAS THE ORGANIST for her Presbyterian church in East Texas and rode a horse into Lindale every Saturday for music lessons. But when she married my dad right after he got out of the service in 1919, she gave up her music. I think that was so painful she barely touched an instrument again except for one time at my absolute prodding when I pushed her into playing the piano at a friend's house. She never really talked about giving up her music, and I wish I had talked to her about that. However, she was such a positive person who never felt that anything was left out of her life and who never found fault. I remember that if we ever came home with a tale of inadequacy on the part of anybody else, she could always find the good.

Mother had this ability to survive through physical and economic crisis. She was always protective of Dad whose health was never good after being gassed in WW I, and she simply worked hard to be sure his life was safe. So when my dad followed the admonition "go west, young man, go west," we moved to a farm in West Texas. I recall when we made a wonderful first cotton crop and it looked like we were going to be out of debt, then on October 29, 1929, the banks closed and there was no money at all. But I remember Mother saying, "We've survived up to this point in time, we'll do fine. We have canned the food and we don't need money to get where we want to go."

Nevertheless when they made that cotton crop, the one thing they did was buy a car because Mother said she would not let her child be educated in a one-room country school. She worked out a deal with this family that had daughters who drove their old Model T to school, and Mother would drive me to their house then I'd go into school with them. It was just a way of her handling a situation that could have been difficult.

Mother – Jessie Henderson at age four   Daughter – Vivian at age four

One of my most vivid school memories is of lunches. In those days children in the country usually went to school with a fried sausage or a slab of ham between a cold biscuit for lunch, but Mother always prepared works of art for me and my two brothers. In the warm weather we'd have lemonade or iced tea or something like that, and we'd have a sandwich with either ground meat or sausage mashed up with homemade relish or dill pickles. And if she had it, there was always a carrot stick, a sliced apple, a hard-boiled egg, and homemade cookies. So opening our lunch box was like opening a magic box.

Mother was such a strong advocate of education. I remember I learned to read by lying on the floor with my elbows on the newspaper and tracing the letters then asking her what they were. And she in her busy life always took the time to look over my shoulder and explain them to me. Now in those days we had abundant love but no money, yet Mother always said "when" not "if" you go to college. She held me close yet at the same time threw me out because she wanted to be sure I could function in the wider world.

Mother – Jessie Anderson at age fifty-seven

Daughter – Vivian Castleberry at age fifty-seven

Last night I awoke thinking about how significant my mother's hands are to me, and I could see them in almost every relationship imaginable. Her youngest sister, Mildred, had polio, and Mother used to recall the times when it was her responsibility to massage those legs before her sister went out to play. So that is one image of her hands. And I see Mother's hands when we were children and lived on the farm. There were no modern conveniences, not even electricity, so I see her hands wringing the overalls, shucking the corn, shelling the peas, snapping the beans, pulling the carrots, pulling the onions.

And I remember another thing about her hands. Mother and Dad had a wonderful relationship, and as I look back on life I remember I never saw the two of them pass without touching each other. I had no idea at that time what this was doing for me, but the love and appreciation they had for each other was transforming me into a woman who, when I was grown up, had no trouble being a sexual person.

And after I had grown, gotten married, and had children, we never arrived at Mother's house that she was not at the car to meet us, whenever that was, and was always reaching for the children. Even before I could get the car door open, Mother's hands were reaching out. So again Mother's hands are a direct extension of so much.

Mother died in her sixties with her first heart attack. She died when my youngest child was three years old, and honestly I went through a period of anger. There were days, even as late as three or four years later, when something would happen in my life and I would pick up the phone and start to call her, but halfway through dialing the number I would remember she wasn't going to answer. As I look at her death since then, I realize I have since moved into the role of mother because she had taught me how. And now I can see my daughters becoming the mother, and I have to tell you it feels good.

My relationships are the beauty that Mother gave me. She was just as wonderful as I always thought she was, and it took me a while to say that because we're not taught to say that. We're taught to look for the controversies in relationships. Her legacy then is total acceptance.

We were a farm family, and Mother cooked on a wood stove in my early childhood. Mother was a creative cook, adding a dab of this and a whiff of that to her recipes.

Chicken Fried Steak

2 lbs. round steak
1 ½ c. flour seasoned with salt and pepper and thoroughly mixed
(Sometimes Mother added garlic powder and paprika to the seasonings, and sometimes she also added ½ cup finely crushed cereal)
Buttermilk, canned milk, or sweet milk
Shortening for frying (in the early days, we used lard;
 Mother preferred Crisco)

Pound steak with a meat cleaver until thin. Place in a bowl and pour milk over it. (Mother preferred buttermilk, but the other choices will do.) Turn meat to saturate all parts. Sift seasoned flour onto wax paper or a large platter and spread to make a thin layer. In a medium to large skillet put shortening. Heat until a pinch of flour dropped into it sizzles. With a fork, lift steak pieces onto seasoned flour (reserve flour not used). Turn until all surfaces of steak are coated. With fingers, press remaining flour into meat. Put steaks into sizzling fat. When lightly browned, turn meat and cook on other side. Remove to a hot platter and keep warm.

Cream Gravy

Pour shortening from steak pan until only 4 tablespoons remain. Add 8 tablespoons flour using leftover from steak batter (tiny fragments of meat enrich gravy). Stir constantly while lightly browning. Stir in 2 cups milk (we use the leftover milk in which steak has been marinated), more if needed, and cook to desired thickness. Add salt and pepper if needed to season.

Mother Soup

To us the only soup worth eating was Mother's four-ingredient variety. It is a family tradition. When under stress or sick, my five daughters and their children sometimes call and ask for some TLC and Mother Soup.

6 small to medium sized potatoes, peeled and chopped
2 c. okra, sliced thin
1 large can tomatoes, chopped (we used 1 qt. home-canned tomatoes)
1 very large or 2 medium-sized onions, peeled and chopped
3 c. chicken broth or water
2 Tbsp. salad oil
1 tsp. salt
Pepper to taste if desired
1 c. water
½ c. flour

Prepare vegetables and set aside. In a large pot, bring chicken broth or water to a gentle boil. Add vegetables, salad oil, salt, and pepper. Cover pot and boil gently until vegetables are tender (about 30 minutes). In a small bowl, mix flour with water and stir until smooth. Add 4 tablespoons soup into mixture and stir well. Slowly add mixture to boiling soup, stirring as you add and being careful not to scald hands. When soup thickens to desired consistency, stop adding mixture and toss the remainder. Continue stirring and boiling for another couple of minutes. Remove from burner. Cover and, if time allows, let soup sit for up to 30 minutes to blend flavors. Serve hot with crackers or corn bread.

Mayonnaise Cake

    2 c. flour
    1 c. sugar
    1 ½ tsp. baking powder
    1 tsp. baking soda
    1 c. mayonnaise
    1 tsp. vanilla
    1 c. water
    1 tsp. salt

Sift flour, sugar, baking powder, soda, and salt into a bowl. In another bowl, mix water, vanilla, and mayonnaise. Stir into dry ingredients. Mix well. Pour into greased baking pan. Bake 30 minutes at 300 degrees. Remove from oven and let cool. Using ice pick, punch cake full of holes.

Glaze for Mayonnaise Cake

    2 c. confectioner's sugar
    2 Tbsp. melted butter
    1 tsp. vanilla
    Canned milk or cream

Stir only enough milk into sugar to make of spreading consistency. Add butter and vanilla. Mix and pour over cooled cake. It will make a glaze. Cut into liberal-sized squares and serve.

Mother's Angel Food Cake

When I was a child, Mother almost always made an angel food cake on Saturdays to serve as Sunday dessert. I sifted the flour/sugar mixture into the batter while she hand-whipped the eggs. It was such a special time because we talked as we worked.

    1 c. flour
    1 ½ c. fine grain sugar
    Few grains of salt
    12 large eggs, whites only
    1 Tbsp. water
    1 tsp. cream of tartar
    1 ½ tsp. vanilla
    ½ tsp. almond extract

Mix flour, sugar, and salt and sift together six times. Set aside. Break eggs and separate, being careful not to get any of the yolk into the whites. Set yolks aside, gently cover with cool water, cover, and refrigerate to use in something else. Beat egg whites until foamy. (Mother beat them by hand. I use a rotary beater.) Add cream of tartar and water. Continue beating until whites begin to thicken. Sprinkle flour/sugar mixture into whites 1 *table-spoon at a time* until all is used, beating and folding until batter looks like smooth white satin. Add flavorings. Pour batter into ungreased tube pan. Bake in 350-degree oven for 50 minutes.

Chicken and Dumplings

Cut a large fryer (3 pounds or more) into serving pieces and boil in 3 quarts seasoned (salt and pepper) water until tender. Remove chicken from broth. In a large bowl, sift 2 to 3 cups flour and ½ teaspoon baking powder. Cut in 3 tablespoons butter or margarine. Add milk to seasoned flour to make a thick dough. Turn out on a floured board and knead. Roll to ¼- to ⅓-inch thickness. With a knife, cut dough into strips and then cut strips across to form pieces 2 to 3 inches long. Lift pieces one at a time into boiling broth. Season to taste with salt and pepper. Gently boil for 10 to 15 minutes. Dish up into a large bowl. Top with chicken pieces or serve separately.

Corn Bread Dressing

4 c. crumbled corn bread
4 c. crumbled biscuits
4 slices whole wheat bread
½ c. melted butter
1 qt. chicken broth or hot water
2 c. chopped sautéed onion (use some green onions with tops)
2 c. chopped sautéed celery
8 hard-cooked eggs, peeled and chopped
1 c. (or less) chopped cooked gizzard if desired
Salt, pepper, and sage (if desired) to taste

Crumble breads and mix with clean hands. In a skillet, sauté onions and celery in the butter. Peel and chop eggs. Chop gizzards very fine. Put onion mixture into bread crumbs and stir to mix. Add broth and/or water until mixture is very moist but not runny. Add boiled eggs. Season with salt, pepper, and sage. Pour into a greased baking dish and bake in 400-degree oven until golden brown, around 45 minutes to an hour depending on thickness of dressing in pan.

Vivian Castleberry

One of my favorite words is grace. When spoken this ordered combination of characters stands alone in summation of that which brings goodness to life. Definitively it includes charm of form or expression, a sense of what is right and proper, thoughtfulness towards others, and goodwill. I selected this term in connection with Vivian Anderson Castleberry for she glows with grace.

This wordsmith proved soulful and good natured as she shared recollections of her mother that captured the comfort in their relationship. Through descriptions of her mother's generosity, Vivian offered hints into her own nature, a nature only partially represented by career and recognition.

Vivian married Curtis Wales Castleberry in 1946 and together they offered the world six children—five daughters and one son who was lost in infancy. While family was first and foremost, Vivian nevertheless answered the calls to write and to help others.

Vivian was women's editor of the *Dallas Times Herald* for twenty-eight years (1955-1984), and during that time she managed the features section of the newspaper, reported, wrote, and edited. She was the first woman in Dallas named to an editorial board of a major newspaper as her strength lay in recognizing and reporting on issues that had an impact on the lives of women and families.

It is that element of her work—women's issues—which carried over into the community. She has been on the board of many organizations that address women's issues and has proven instrumental in various other such arenas. She is a founder of the Women's Center of Dallas, the Women's Issues Network, and the Dallas Women's Foundation. She helped create the Family Place, the first shelter in Dallas for victims of spousal abuse. She served on both the Dallas and Texas Commission on the Status of Women, and on the advisory committee for the SMU Symposium on the Education of Women for Social and Political Leadership.

Her efforts reflect a faculty for knowing what constitutes a positive and proactive public agent and have been affirmed through various awards and honors. She was named to the Texas Women's Hall of Fame (1984) and honored by the Washington, D.C. Press Club Foundation (1988) as a "change agent in America for the coverage of women's news." One of her

Vivian Castleberry

most prestigious honors came when the Association of Women Journalists named its Woman of Courage and its annual scholarship awards the Vivian Castleberry Awards. She has also been honored for her talents as a journalist and public servant with the Louise B. Raggio Award (1988) given by the Dallas/Fort Worth National Association of Women Business Owners.

Since retirement in 1984, Vivian's life has remained richly rewarding. She has made three trips to the Soviet Union (before and after the fall of communism) as a grassroots citizen diplomat. She has written and published a book, *Daughters of Dallas*. She has chaired an International Women's Peace Conference at SMU (her alma mater) and the Power of Positive Parenting Conference. Recently she received an honorary Doctor of Humane Letters degree from SMU, but perhaps the most fitting award came when she was named Texas Mother of the Year in 1996.

Throughout a lifetime of extraordinary accomplishments with family, journalism, and community service, Vivian Anderson Castleberry remains ever the figure of grace.

Becky Chavarría-Cháirez

public and media relations; broadcast journalist

Bertha M. Chavarría

b. 1931

My mother is a beautiful person. In high school she was the queen of the prom, and when I see her I think of Audrey Hepburn in Roman Holiday *—just an innocent beauty with a fragile soul.*

BECAUSE I'M AN INFORMATION GATHERER, I have retained a lot from my mother and tried to piece together the why's that gave her such a resourceful nature. I guess if you stop and think, you see it has a lot to do with when she was born and the conditions she lived under during the Depression.

How her family managed to eat at all during those years is interesting. There was a relative who lived with them and worked in a restaurant kitchen, and whenever food was left over they'd let him take it home. So Mother said that what he brought home was eaten and that's how they existed. There was no such thing as going to buy groceries, and they didn't believe in getting any kind of government aid. So where did their resourcefulness come from? I guess from their hunger.

My mother is a very small person and that goes back to the Depression. Even though she was born full term, she weighed less than five pounds because her mother didn't have any vitamins or calcium. My mother was so tiny she could fit in a little shoebox, so that is one image to connect with her. During the Depression there wasn't enough money to buy good shoes for the kids, and because Mother was not the oldest her shoes had already been

Bertha M. Chavarría

65

Bertha Malacara, age 8, at First Holy Communion at San Fernando Cathedral, San Antonio, May 1939

worn. I remember when I was a child we'd go buy shoes at the downtown Joskes in San Antonio, and I used to think Mother bought me the more expensive shoes because I was such a little princess. Mother would say, "You must always wear a good and well-fitted pair of shoes. You must take care of your feet and protect them and keep them clean. And never share your shoes with anyone." As I got older, I realized Mother's particular shoe requirements were a vestige of the Depression years.

Mother has always been practical and sensible. She keeps herself busy with the family, and her work is all very home based since the house is her world and all she has mastered is within that sphere. She is very much in command and has been the authoritarian figure who stayed home and reared us. She did a lot of things for me and my sister—curtains for our rooms, our clothing—yet even though we had the money to buy these things, she would say she was just saving money.

Mother is very artistic, very talented, and that is also part of her legacy. She can make something out of nothing. Things that people throw on the sidewalk, Mother can find a use for. And of course, she can take an outfit and transform it into something totally different. She has this fine ability with her hands to sew and do fine work, but the images I have of her using her hands wouldn't just be of her sewing, it would also be of her cooking.

Mother's kitchen symbolizes her journey of assimilation. Her mother's generation came from a time when recipes were never written down but were passed on with hands-on lessons. Sometimes it took a lifetime to master or come close to re-creating an old family recipe. Her mother—who never taught my mother to cook—didn't have measuring cups and spoons

Bertha Malacara, age 15, first "formal" dance at Elks Club, 1946 photo by Corona Studio

Bertha Malacara, age 19, queen of the senior prom at St. Henry's Academy in San Antonio, May 1950

since in those days one learned to cook by throwing a pinch, a smidge, a generous dash of this and that into the pot or skillet.

But my mother was just the opposite. In teaching herself how to cook she followed recipes in minute detail, and once she felt she had mastered something, the real recipe tweaking would begin. I remember on Sunday mornings before we'd get dressed for church I'd watch my mother use the *molcajete* to stone grind her garlic and spices. Then when it was time to get dressed, she'd put on Shalimar perfume and we'd leave. I remember I would hold her hand in church and could still smell the garlic and spices mixed with her Shalimar and I'd think to myself, "Oh, that smells so good."

Now if you were to ask family and friends for Mother's trademark recipe it would be her fruitcake. She'd often begin her fruitcake mission in late October when little by little she'd buy the ingredients, always hunting for bargains and the best of everything. Many years we'd spend a Friday evening or Saturday morning shelling pecans from our backyard until she had enough nuts for cooking. From year to year, her fruitcakes were a little different, like the vintner's annual fruits of his labor, and they were always made by the same loving, confident, and creative hands.

As I said, I've tried to figure out what Mother's all about, and the other day I was watching *Snow White and the Seven Dwarfs* and realized I might have discovered the Rosetta stone of my mother's life. It has to be that movie. It was released in 1937 when Mother was about seven years old, and I suspect it left a life-long impression on her at a time when she was young and grappling with assimilating as a first-generation Mexican American girl.

I see the scene of Snow White sweeping the dwarfs' cabin, and I see my mother sweeping the house. I see Snow White's tears, and I feel my mother's presence. I hear Snow White's laugh, and I hear my Mother's laugh. Mother would sing songs from the movie to us when I was young, and she had that tiny falsetto, soprano-like Snow White tone as she'd "hum a merry tune" while working. I remember as a child she would tell me, "You have to eat your beets because that's why Snow White had such rosy cheeks." And when Snow White says goodnight to the dwarfs, she kisses each on the head, and that was our ritual with the only difference being that Mother would take her hand and make a sign of the cross over us. So as I try to figure out the things in life that impressed upon Mother to be a certain way, I see a lot in that film.

The fondest time I have with Mother is when she talks about her parents because she's sharing with me something that is so private, so intimate.

Fruitcake

I egg
I c. water (at room temperature)
I pkg. Pillsbury Date Bread Mix (add spices to dry mix)
I tsp. cinnamon
½ tsp. nutmeg
¼ tsp. allspice
I ½ Tbsp. vegetable oil
I ½ c. chopped pecans
I c. raisins
I c. candied cherries
½ c. candied pineapple

Heat oven to 325 degrees. Grease and flour a 9 x 5 x 3 inch loaf pan. Combine bread mix with spices. Mix in water. Add egg and all remaining ingredients. Stir by hand until well combined. Pour into pan. Before baking, decorate top of cake with cherry and pecan halves. Bake about 1 hour and 20 minutes or until a toothpick inserted in center comes out clean. Cool in pan for 30 minutes before removing. Cool thoroughly. Wrap with gauze dipped in brandy, and sponge the brandy onto the loaf. Wrap and refrigerate in aluminum foil. Soak once a week. It is best to soak cake about two weeks or longer. For a moist cake place about 1 inch of water in a shallow baking pan on the lower oven rack. Remove 15 minutes before cake is done. You may double the recipe and fix two loaves at one time, or separate. The double mixture is very hard to stir.

Tongue

1 3-lb. beef tongue
2 tsp. salt
3 bay leaves
1 onion, sliced
1 carrot, sliced
1 stalk celery, sliced
1 Tbsp. pickling spice

Wash tongue; cover with hot water. Add seasonings and vegetables. Cook for 3 hours or until very tender. Cool in liquid. Trim excess tissue from root end; remove skin. Slice and serve.

Salmon Loaf

1 can (14¾ oz.) Honey Boy pink salmon
2 c. soft bread crumbs (1½ slices of bread, let sit uncovered
   to help crumble the bread)
⅓ c. finely minced onion
¼ c. milk
2 eggs
2 Tbsp. minced parsley
1 Tbsp. fresh lemon juice
¼ tsp. each of salt and dill weed
Dash of black pepper

Drain salmon, reserving 2 tablespoons of liquid; flake. Combine all ingredients. Place in well-greased 8½ x 4½ x 2½ inch loaf pan. Bake at 350 degrees for 45 minutes. Serves 4 to 6.

Oatmeal

1 ½ c. whole milk
¾ c. oats
Dash of salt
2 tsp. sugar
1 tsp. cinnamon

Boil milk. Stir in oats with rest of ingredients. Cook on medium heat until oats are soft. This makes a small serving.

Becky Chavarría-Cháirez

There are people blessed with the ability to juggle a multitude of projects and responsibilities at once, and Becky Chavarría-Cháirez is such a woman. She has a capacity for taking an idea from its genesis to full growth. She has the enthusiasm to maintain a demanding lifestyle. And she has the organizational skills to run the country.

Yet there is another side to Becky. There is the soft, compassionate Becky who helps those who have not been as blessed in life as she. There is the humorous Becky who gleans joy from gatherings. And there is the personable Becky who has a great fondness for friends and family.

Becky has served in various roles in broadcasting. She began her career at KTSA/KTFM Radio in San Antonio, Texas, as news anchor and public service director and has also been the morning news co-anchor, public affairs director, and Dallas bureau chief for WBAP/KSCS Radio. In addition Becky has held public relations, promotions, and membership positions with Arthur Young & Company, Pavlik and Associates, KLIF Radio, and The Science Place. Recently she has been a special contributor to *La Vida* on WFAA-TV Channel 8 and a radio commentator and live talk show host on KERA-FM, the Dallas NPR affiliate.

As special public/media relations consultant for Hispanic markets for Southwest Organ Bank, her efforts brought such success that they have been replicated throughout the Southwest. Prior to joining Southwest Organ Bank, Becky was promotions director at KESS Radio, a Spanish-language station in Dallas for which she designed, promoted, and implemented all contests, public/community relations, and special projects.

Becky Chavarría-Cháirez

Ms. Chavarría-Cháirez' portfolio also includes the fields of public and media relations. She is founder and owner of a company specializing in cross-cultural communications for Hispanic and mainstream markets, Catchphrase PR. She also owns The Arts Coach®, a firm providing management consulting and one-on-one professional mentorship to arts leaders.

Apart from the aforementioned, Becky is noted as a freelance journalist, self-syndicated editorial writer, and author. Her editorials and feature articles have appeared in the *Dallas Business Journal*, *Dallas Morning News*, *La Fuente*, *San Antonio Express-News*, and *San Francisco Chronicle* to name a few. Becky also has written a children's book, *Magda Madrigal*, published by Arte Público Press.

Throughout her career Becky's fund-raising efforts have assisted dozens of groups such as Girls Incorporated of Metropolitan Dallas, The Hispanic 50, The Hockaday School, Pegasus Theater, Victims Outreach, and Volunteer of America.

When all is said and done, Becky Chavarría-Cháirez places all the roles she plays into a balanced life with great personal flair.

Eileen Marie Collins

astronaut; colonel, USAF

Eileen Collins and mother, Rose Marie Collins, 1993

Rose Marie Collins

b. 1927

My mother tends to be kind of impulsive, like the day she came home with a blue Gremlin. I remember looking out the window and saying to myself, "I will never be able to face my friends for the rest of my life." Of course, I was a teenager and all I cared about was how the back of the car was just chopped off. But she loved that car.

MOTHER WAS TWENTY-SIX YEARS OLD when she got married to my father, then she had my brother when she was twenty-seven. I was born when she was twenty-eight and then my sister came along when Mother was twenty-nine. So she had three kids, one right after the other, and after that she went through a miscarriage and one stillborn child before my little brother—who is six years younger than me—was born.

Then when I was about nine years old my dad was in the hospital, and that was when my mother went to work as a stenographer in the parole office at a prison where she had worked before she was married. She would tell us kids she really didn't want to work and would rather be home because that was where she belonged. She always talked about how, out of all of our friends, she was the only mother who worked and how sad she was about that. But to be honest, I think she enjoyed getting out of the house.

Rose Marie Collins and daughter, Eileen Collins, 1992

I used to say to her, even when I was a kid, "Mom, I think you're happier having a job." She worked with five or six other women, and I used to hear all about them and the things that were going on at work. So to help her out, I would try to have dinner cooked or the snow shoveled or the lawn cut. And actually all of us kids had little chores around the house that we always did to help out.

But you know, even though Mother worked she was always there for us after she would get home in the afternoon, and that was fine with me. I guess what I want to say right here is that mothers who work shouldn't feel guilty. My mother needed to get out of the house, and having a job was right for her. Like I said, she was still able to be home every night, and if I needed to talk to her about something, it was okay for me to just wait until she was finished at the job.

Mother is a little bit of a lot of things. I hate to just give her one label to identify what I think she is mostly, but I guess if I did I would say that first she is a healer. When we were sick as kids she was great. We'd get on the couch and she'd get us ginger ale and put a blanket on us and turn on the television. So we all liked being sick because she would call in to work and take the day off, and we would have her at home with us. So she's a nurse in a way, tending our wounds.

I also can see her as an achiever, a leader, and a teacher. Those characteristics definitely apply, but above them all, the role as a great mom is probably the one that applies the very best. She is a little bit of everything, so that is who I would say she is identity wise—the greatest mom. You know, I've thanked her for lots of individual things she's done for me, but I don't think I've ever said to her that I think she's the "greatest mom" except maybe when I was a little kid. So I guess I'd like to say now to my mom that I think the things she has done and does for me are really good, and I think she is truly the greatest mom anyone could ask for.

Rose Marie Collins, daughter, Eileen Collins, and granddaughter, 1999

When I'm asked in an interview about who my role models are, I always say my mother and my father, and that is the truth. I say that because if parents hear my interview, then hopefully they'll see that they are or can be a role model for their kids. You don't have to be a famous athlete or a movie star to be a role model to your kids. And that's the point I want to drive home.

So if I were to try to pinpoint her legacy, it would have to be a combination of things. A combination of strength, of positiveness, of independence. There were times when my father was sick, and she was real positive in getting us through that. There was the time her good friend died of cancer, and again she found the positive in that because after everything was over she talked about how glad she was that her friend wasn't suffering anymore.

And I think that another of her strong characteristics might be her independence. She's not a dependent type of person at all. If she needs something done, she can get it done herself. And I admire that because you know way back in the days when I was young, lots of women just really weren't like that. I definitely think my independent nature is tied in with my mother's.

My mom came from a middle-class family. Her father was Irish and worked for the railroad, and her mother, Augusta Fromm, was German. But I never knew either one of them because they both died before I was born. Well Mom didn't have a lot of privileges like piano or modeling or sewing lessons or things like that. But that is another thing about her being a good mom because she sent us kids to summer camp and made sure my sister and I went to sewing and modeling lessons. None of my friends did that kind of stuff, but my mom said she wanted us to know it and I'm glad she did.

Another thing she did every year was take all four of us kids on weeklong vacations while my father was away working in Rochester. We might drive to the Virginia beach or go to Niagara Falls or somewhere, and that was a loving effort on my mother's part.

She is a good mother, and since I believe that no one's perfect, I would never say she's perfect but I would say she is honest. And she has always told us she loves us. I remember she would always be sure to say, "I don't love one of you kids more than the other, and you can always come and talk to me about anything."

Another thing, my mother always stood by her rules. I remember one time, probably in my later high school years, my mother insisted I be home at a certain time on the weekends. I revolted against that but she didn't back down. She just said, "If I didn't love you, I'd let you stay out all night, but because I do love you, I want you home when I tell you." Now I was furious, but I came home on time.

When I decided I wanted to go into flying, Mother was supportive and I believe a lot of the confidence I have is because I have always felt that if I ever need her she'll be there. I have a comfortable relationship with my mother and we talk about everything, and I have always felt loved and supported.

My mother represents a person who is goodness and wholesomeness. She's a real person who says whatever comes to her mind, but it's hard to recall the things she has said to me because there are just so many. So what does my mother mean to me? Everything!

I don't really have many recipes I can give you because basically this describes my mother—meatloaf. Ground beef, egg, milk, chop up some onions, throw in some bread crumbs, tomato sauce, mix it up with your hands. I mean, she didn't have recipes, she just threw things in.

Meat Loaf

1 lb. ground sirloin
2 eggs
Bread crumbs
Chopped onion
Salt and pepper
1 can Hunt's tomato sauce

Mix well, form into loaf, sprinkle Durkee's French Fried onions on top. Bake for 45 minutes to 1 hour in a 350-degree oven.

Eileen Marie Collins

As I drove through the gates, past the guardhouse, and into the Lyndon Baines Johnson Houston Space Center, I couldn't help but smile. The last time I stepped foot on these grounds was back in July of 1969, the summer before my senior year at Clear Creek High School when I had been selected as a teletypist to send stories of the Apollo 11 space flight to an English newspaper. I was awed by NASA then, and some thirty years later I again experienced that sense. Today however my awe was also due in part to the upcoming interview with Colonel Eileen Marie Collins, USAF.

As I sat across the table from Eileen, I found her to be a levelheaded, no-holds-barred woman who dove right into the interview about her mother in order to maximize the hour she could take out of her schedule. After listening to a question, she would most often pause then offer a candid and direct answer, yet there were many instances where Eileen traveled back and forth between humor and solemnity.

Eileen Marie Collins USAF, 1998
Photo courtesy NASA

A native of New York, Eileen Marie Collins knew early on she wanted to be a pilot. To achieve her goal, she first received an associate degree in science and mathematics and a B.A. in mathematics and economics. She also received an M.S. in operations research and an M.A. in space systems management. Later she graduated from Air Force Undergraduate Pilot Training in Oklahoma and was a T-38 instructor pilot. From 1983 to 1985 she was a C-141 aircraft commander and instructor pilot at Travis Air Force Base in California then spent the following year as a student with the Air Force Institute of Technology before being assigned to the U.S. Air Force Academy in Colorado as an assistant professor in mathematics and a T-41 instructor pilot.

In 1990 she was selected for NASA's astronaut program and attained that position in 1991. She has been assigned to Orbiter with various responsibilities, worked in Mission Control for numerous shuttle missions, and served as the Astronaut Office Spacecraft Systems Branch Chief. A veteran of three space flights, Eileen has logged over five hundred and thirty-seven hours in space. She served as pilot on STS-63 in 1995 and STS-84 in 1997, and was the first woman shuttle commander on STS-93 in 1999.

Colonel Collins has built an impressive list of accomplishments, yet during the interview Eileen clearly credited much of what she has achieved to her mother, Rose Marie Collins, for passing along a legacy of strength, positiveness, and independence through love and example. And I must say I do believe this daughter, Eileen Marie Collins, will pass on her own legacy to science and society.

Ann Louise Shaw Conradt

b. 1920

If I were to thank my mom, it would be for being supportive, for making me feel like whatever I pursued was okay, for her total acceptance of my being what I want to be and how I want to be.

Jody Conradt and mother, Ann Louise Shaw Conradt

WHAT IS IMPORTANT TO HER, and people say this a lot, is family. That's what her life is and I think she would say her greatest gift is the legacy of her children. I don't know why little things stick out, but I remember one time Dad saying to Mom, "We have the best kids in the world. Nobody could have better kids than the ones we have." I think their whole life has been to support and help whatever we're going to do. Now we didn't have what I would call mother-and-daughter talks, but there was unspoken communication where I knew what was expected. I knew what was right and wrong, and I didn't want to do anything to disappoint her.

I always knew Mom would do whatever it took if I asked. I can look back and think of the many sacrifices she—as well as my father—made to give me opportunities, but they never said, "Well you're out there doing that, and we've had to give up this so you can do it." There was never that. When it came time for me to go to college, it was assumed I'd go to Baylor, but they really didn't have the money so I don't know where it came from. Overall I just know I never felt like I didn't have everything the other Baylor students had.

My mother is giving and I know you're going to think we're fixated on this, but in a small town how do you show your compassion? You cook for people. You cook when there's a funeral, when there's a wedding, whenever something's going on. And she is happy cooking, and that's how she finds a lot of gratification. Most of her recipes come from her mother, and my mother prides herself in her cooking as I think a lot of women at that point in time did. It was a time when you'd have three meals including dessert, and that's how I grew up.

Food was always central, and Mother always hosted everybody on both

Ann Louise Shaw

sides of the family. She would start cooking days before a get-together, and I remember her getting up early in the morning and starting whatever she was going to prepare. I could smell it and I could hear her rattling around. Now I didn't get too involved in the cooking, but I remember her kneading the dough and letting it sit, so I at least know the whole process. I watched her any number of times, so making bread is probably—if I had to pull out an image—the one thing I see her doing with her hands. And the interesting thing is she cooks everybody's favorites. If I were to go home for a Sunday dinner and my two nieces and nephews were to also come, she'd have everybody's favorite foods. That's just her nature, so my mother's kindness is like always having your favorite meal.

I've often wondered what there was in a small town to drive her to balance so many things with such diligence. Mother didn't have the opportunity to go to college, and I've wondered what profession she would have chosen if she could have. There's no doubt in my mind she's bright enough, competitive enough to have done just about anything. And she's just so diligent. That's the best word I can come up with. Whatever she tackled, she tackled. I think about her diligence and how it might be a small or a big task, but she attacks either as if it might be the last thing she's going to do.

Now one thing she really tackled was sewing. Maybe it was a financial issue or the fact that there weren't too many places in town to buy clothes, but she made almost everything I wore. That's also something I see her doing with her hands. She was a meticulous seamstress who made her own patterns. She's definitely what I'd consider a perfectionist because if something didn't turn out exactly right, she'd mutter to herself then rip it out and do it again. And she'd stay up late if she had to because she was so determined it was going to be right. Sometimes my dad would get irritated because our house was small and the sewing machine was right in the middle of everything. But I came to realize how driven she was because it was like she was thinking to herself, "I'm doing this and it doesn't matter if he gets irritated."

Now I think my mom and I share a passionate spirit. My earliest recollections of her—besides being a mom and doing things that moms do—is

Ann Louise Shaw Conradt, 1998

81

of her playing in a softball league. I must have been four or five years old, but I remember thinking how neat it was she could do that. She played third base, and I can still see her in her yellow T-shirt, jeans with the legs rolled up, and a baseball cap. I remember her assuming that athletic position at third base where she'd be down and ready for the ball to be hit to her. So I saw her playing and assumed everybody's mom played baseball. I think it was just a given I'd be involved in sports, and I was really shocked when I got out of that town and realized that not everybody was having the same experiences.

I think my mom would have been the kind of person I would like to have been on a team with because she has the qualities that make good team members—she's competitive, focused, and hard working. To this day when she comes to our women's basketball games at the University of Texas, I see how she puts on her serious game face. In line with that, Mother at seventy-nine golfs every day and is passionate about that. She gets up in the morning to go out to the course, and if there happens to be another guy or two out there then she plays with them, but if not it doesn't matter. She just plays because for Mom golf is simply about making the next shot.

What I admire most about my mother is that for a woman from her era she's
really independent. She enjoys life and has found ways to channel her
energy that are rewarding and fulfilling.

Salmon Patties

1 7¾-oz. can pink salmon
1 egg
¼ c. minced onion
¼ c. flour
¼ c. cornmeal
1½ tsp. baking powder
Oil to fry in

Remove bones and dark meat from salmon if desired. Add all other ingredients. Mixture will be sticky. Drop and form round, flat patties in oiled pan. Fry until golden brown.

Corn Casserole

3 Tbsp. milk
3 Tbsp. butter
3 Tbsp. sugar
3 eggs
2 cans corn
¼ minced onion
¼ c. bell pepper
¼ c. pimientos

Mix all ingredients and bake 30 minutes at 350 degrees.

Easy Refrigerator Rolls

2 c. warm water
2 pkg. active dry yeast
½ c. sugar
2 tsp. salt
6½-7 c. flour
I egg
¼ c. shortening

Dissolve yeast in warm water. Add sugar, salt, and half the flour. Add egg and shortening. Mix in remaining flour with spoon or hand until dough is easy to handle. Place greased side up in a greased bowl. Cover with aluminum foil. Place in refrigerator. Punch down occasionally as dough rises. About 2 hours before baking, shape into rolls. Cover with cloth and let rise until double in size. Bake in 350-degree oven until golden brown. *(Can be made into rolls before putting in refrigerator if you like. Let rise until double in size and bake.)*

Coconut Cream Pie

3 egg yolks
⅔ c. sugar
⅓ c. flour (rounded)
2 c. milk
I tsp. vanilla
I c. coconut
I Tbsp. butter or oleo
¼ tsp. salt

Put egg yolks, sugar, ¼ cup milk, and salt in blender and blend. In pan on stove, put 1¾ cup milk and butter. Just before milk boils, add blender ingredients, stirring until thickened. Add coconut and vanilla. Cool and pour into baked pie shell. Cover top with meringue.

I use this pie filling for chocolate pie. Just add cocoa in blender with other ingredients. Also filling can be used for banana pudding, layering vanilla wafers then bananas with filling.

Meringue

3 egg whites
¼ tsp. cream of tartar
4 Tbsp. sugar

Add cream of tartar to egg whites and beat until stiff; add sugar gradually and continue beating until they stand in points when beater is lifted. Spread over pie and bake at 325 degrees until browned and firm, about 20-25 minutes.

Jody Conradt

Finding a parking spot on the University of Texas campus in Austin was not a difficult task this day. Since I was interviewing the head women's basketball coach, I was given a parking pass that placed me within one hundred feet of the athletic offices. I entered the building, climbed the stairs, took the elevator up, and met Barb Kowal, media relations director for women's athletics. Barb showed me to Ms. Conradt's office and apologized for the disarray from remodeling. But it was this chaos that provided an icebreaker for the interview with the nationally recognized college-level head women's basketball coach, Jody Conradt.

Within seconds Ms. Conradt appeared. The grin on her face was elfin, the gait in her step assured, and the grip of her handshake solid. Stepping around crates overflowing with folders, Jody took a seat at her makeshift workstation. Unrattled by the disorder, she revealed an important facet of her nature—the ability to find order in chaos. Perhaps, I mused, *that* is her key to success and then I recalled what others credit her success to—talent, determination, take-charge attitude, dedication—and Jody Conradt's complexity rushed front and center.

Jody Conradt and mother, Ann Louise Shaw Conradt, 1998

Jody was born and reared in the small Texas town of Goldthwaite where she later gained athletic notice by averaging forty points a game for the girls basketball team. After high school she attended Baylor University in Waco and earned a degree in physical education. From there she pursued teaching and coaching at Waco Midway High School before returning to Baylor to earn a master's degree. In 1969 Jody coached basketball, volleyball, and track at Sam Houston State University in Huntsville and four years later joined the staff at the University of Texas in Arlington to coach basketball, volleyball, and softball. In 1976 Jody took over the basketball and volleyball programs at the University of Texas in Austin and her notoriety grew exponentially.

Her honors are numerous: all-time-winningest women's basketball coach in history; six-time National Coach of the Year; only the eighth coach in Division I men's and women's basketball history (and the first and only women's basketball coach) to reach the illustrious 700-career victory milestone; five-time Southwest Conference Coach of the Year;

International Women's Sports Hall of Fame Inductee; future Texas Sports Hall of Fame Inductee; and Texas Women's Hall of Fame Inductee.

And at the apex of her honors is the induction into the Naismith National Memorial Basketball Hall of Fame in 1998. With that induction, Jody became just the second women's basketball coach to receive that honor. Recently she has been nominated for the Naismith College Women's Basketball Coach of the 20th Century.

It seems fitting that this Texas daughter, who praised the passionate and competitive spirit of her mother, Ann Conradt, can lay claim to the adage that "the apple doesn't fall too far from the tree."

Wilhelmina Delco

Wilhelmina Delco and mother, Juanita Heath Fitzgerald Watson

Juanita Heath Fitzgerald Watson

b. 1911

When Mother died she had been in such pain I was glad for her to get relief. Mother was convinced that God was waiting for her and she went peacefully. My husband closed her eyes and I said a prayer. I said, "Mother, rest in peace; you've earned your rest."

I NEVER STOOD IN AWE of my mother except once. To explain, when I went to college I was going South for the first time and my stepfather didn't really want me to go, but I went to Fisk in Nashville. So my mother, grandfather, and I went to Nashville, and were all pleasantly surprised because we didn't have any idea what college would be like. They went back and I only came home usually for Christmas, but I didn't make it home my senior year.

Juanita Heath Fitzgerald Watson

Anyway, I didn't see Mother that Christmas, so the next time I was going to see her was at graduation. Now Mother was short and heavier than me, and she had real long hair and wore it in this bun. And she wore these huge, gold earrings—those were my mother's trademark. Well, when I went to the train station, I recognized my grandfather immediately, but I didn't recognize the woman with him. I'll never forget it. This lady had on a black suit, a white blouse, and this little red rose at her neck. She had on this huge black straw hat with this great big red rose on top of it. I kept looking as I walked closer, then I said, "That's Mother!"

She had lost weight and cut her hair. Now she still had on big earrings, but they weren't hoops, they were pearls. I just stood there with my mouth open, and when she got closer she smiled and said, "How about that?" To this day, when I think of Mother getting off that train, that's the one time I stood absolutely flabbergasted. She was so beautiful.

I remember Mother and I were talking one day and I said we were just poor people, and Mother said, "No, we aren't poor, we just don't have any money." I always think of that because it defines her attitude. That was Mother's philosophy, always putting things in the context of how she was going to deal with them. She just had a great sense of balance. For instance, Mother's idea of cleaning was she'd get up Saturday morning and roll up the carpet and put it in the corner. She'd take down the curtains and blinds then tell us kids it was time to clean. Then she'd leave. That's what I mean about a great sense of balance.

Another thing, and I've quoted it often, is one time I came home from school and told Mother someone said, "Sally's mom gave her a nickel for all the A's she made. You never give us any money for grades." All she said was, "Listen, I get up every morning and go to work and get a check, and you get up every morning and go to school and bring home good grades.

And that is my job and this is your job." That I never forgot. All five of her kids not only graduated from high school but also from college. We never even thought about not going to college even if we didn't have any money, because Mother just assumed we'd go.

Another favorite thing I have about Mother was her attitude toward education. When she married, Mother had not graduated from high school, but later she got her G.E.D. and even later, she went to Rutgers. I didn't even know about her going to Rutgers until after she died and my sister came down. It seems Mother had made my sister promise we'd put in her obituary that she had gone to college. See, Mother was strong like that.

Daughter Debbie Agbottah, Wilhelmina Delco, mother, Juanita Watson, daughter Loretta Edelen

Mother was also strong and partisan in politics. She thought it was disgraceful not to vote, not to know who you were voting for, and she'd sit up and quiz people. Mother was very aware of current events and the whole sense of politics and the responsibility to vote and to be involved. And she was not only conscious in that sense, but Mother believed in speaking up, so you always felt you could never hide behind the idea you couldn't do anything about certain situations. She had no qualms and she gave us a keen sense of not only what was going on but also a sense of responsibility to respond. The responsibility to get involved was definitely passed along to me from her.

But through it all Mother didn't do community service. She worked and when she quit working, she quit and never looked back. She was just always deeply immersed in her family. If you were her child, she would take on anything and anybody in defense of you. She knew until the minute she was gone everybody's birthday, anniversary, and graduation, and she had five children, fifteen grandchildren, and fifteen great-grandchildren. She had a fantastic memory.

Mother always was a fighter. She got that attitude growing up in the environment that she did. She was born in New Orleans. Her father worked as a master carpenter for the Illinois Central Railroad, and Chicago was the end of the line. So they moved to Chicago and within a year after they got there, her mother died of appendicitis. She knew she had it but didn't want to stop and do anything about it, so it finally ruptured and she died on the way to the hospital. Mother was just eleven years old, but she got through it because she was a fighter.

In November of 1967 Mother was diagnosed with uterine cancer and given six months to live. That was the worst Christmas we ever had. I just couldn't stop crying, but thankfully she lived. Then in 1979 she was diagnosed with breast cancer and had a mastectomy, but again Mother was a fighter and would exercise even in the hospital because she wanted to survive. She moved to Texas when she was sixty years old and lived until the age of eighty-seven. She lived with me so long and then she got sick and relied on me, and she would say, "I don't tell you often enough, but you know I depend on you." But I knew, I knew. She died on January 26, 1999.

Mother left me with a strong sense of family because she put her family first. Her whole world revolved around her children, and she was protective and supportive and always interested, even in the grandchildren and great-grandchildren. The strongest thing she gave me was that sense of family.

I miss Mother, but I don't mourn her. Every day in my house I still see her and talk to her. I can close my eyes and see my mother at the train station when I graduated from college, I can see her in the kitchen. I can just see her, so she's here, all over, everywhere.

Mother was from Louisiana. She did all the cooking and she was a wonderful cook, but Mother liked to change things so you never were really sure what she was going to have, except her staples.

Candied Sweet Potatoes

4 medium-sized sweet potatoes (canned yams may be used)

Boil until fork tender - drain and peel - slice about ½ inch thick - set aside.

Mix:
6 Tbsp. sugar
1 Tbsp. water
½ c. dark corn syrup
2 Tbsp. vanilla
¼ tsp. orange extract
Cinnamon and nutmeg to taste
½ stick butter or oleo

Bring to boil; simmer until well blended. Pour over sweet potatoes. Bake in 350-degree oven until thoroughly warmed. May be covered with small marshmallows.

Creole Shrimp

1 lb. peeled and deveined shrimp
½ onion
½ green pepper
1 clove garlic
1 stalk celery
1 c. tomatoes (whole or diced)
All-purpose lite salt Creole seasoning

Cook shrimp in small amount of oil until pink. Add onions, green pepper, garlic, and celery; stir until just slightly crisp. Add about ½ cup of flour. Add tomatoes and salt and water to cover. Simmer until well mixed. Serve over steamed rice.

Wilhelmina Ruth Fitzgerald Delco

When I met Wilhelmina Delco for the interview, it was the first time I had the pleasure of her company, and it took only seconds in her presence to understand that Wilhelmina's mother knew what she was doing when she named her first-born child. Her name reverberates with strength and confidence. Pronounce it slowly, firmly—Wilhelmina Ruth Fitzgerald Delco—and you hear its punch, its dynamism.

Over a period of two hours, I drew many conclusions about her multi-faceted personality. As she shared the memories of her mother coupled with information about her own family and role in society, a mosaic became pieced together. On the one hand there was tenderness, strength, humor. On the other, pain, joy, and compassion. There was love and respect, and there was knowledge and perception. There was rationality, ingenuity, and confidence.

Wilhelmina Delco and Gib Lewis
Photo courtesy of Texas House of Representatives

Wilhelmina has dedicated more than three decades to public service. As a concerned parent of four, she became an active participant and leader in her children's schools through roles with the Parent Teacher's Association, the Austin Independent School District's Board of Trustees, and later the Austin Community College Board of Trustees.

However, those roles were just the beginning of her accomplishments. She would go on to be recognized as a force in the political arena. She became the first African American official elected at-large from Travis County, and during her ten terms in the Texas Legislature she served on more than twenty different committees.

By 1979 Wilhelmina was appointed chair of the House Higher Education Committee where she served until 1991 when she was appointed

Wilhelmina Delco
Photo courtesy of Texas House of Representatives

Speaker Pro Tempore—the first woman and second African American in this second highest position in the Texas House—until 1993.

Her efforts toward promoting excellence in education have led to her being awarded honorary doctoral degrees from ten colleges and universities. Numerous scholarships have been named in honor of both Wilhelmina and her husband, Exalton. And as a top honor she was elected to the Texas Women's Hall of Fame in the area of education.

Since her retirement from the Texas Legislature in 1995, Wilhelmina has remained an active force in higher education by serving on a number of national and local boards. She also serves as an adjunct professor at the University of Texas in Austin.

While the aforementioned is but a surface sampling of her involvement and accomplishments, it was enough for me to conclude that Wilhelmina's mother knew what she was doing when she christened her first-born daughter with a name of such strength and presence. This truly is a case where the name does honor to the woman just as the woman—Wilhelmina Ruth Fitzgerald Delco—does honor to the name.

Lillian Dunlap

retired brigadier general, U.S. Army

Mary Lucinda Schermerhorn Dunlap

b. 1895

I guess Mama's legacy is love. Our family loves each other, and you don't see that in a lot of families. I've worked with kids who've never been hugged, who don't know what a hug is, but Mama hugged and she loved.

THERE ARE NO HIDDEN SECRETS ABOUT MAMA. She was a survivor whose parents died when she was young, but Mama's philosophy was you do what you have to and work hard at it. She was born in 1895 and her father died when she was twelve years old. After that she and her mother moved to Austin to live with relatives. Then later Mother went to the University of Texas, and after two years her mother died. At that time you

Baby Lillian and mother, Mary Lucinda Schermerhorn Dunlap

could get a teaching certificate with only two years of education, so one of her brothers-in-law encouraged her to get a teaching job in Mission, Texas. She took his advice and that is where she met Daddy.

Imagine, Mama must have been around nineteen years old and teaching English to big football players who called her Miss Mary. Anyway, my daddy got a crush on her and used to go sit in on her classes. Eventually they fell in love, got married, and lived in Mission for a while and then I was born three years later. When I was six months old we moved to San Antonio, and Mama stopped working and started our big family. See, I was born in 1922, my sister Lucille twenty-five months after me, Dorothy three years after her, Mary Bess twenty months after her, and Carolyn six years after her.

I don't think of Mama as unique; she was just what we think a mother should be, and she was a good mother who gave us an ethical grounding and a sense of discipline. I wouldn't say we were ideal kids, but we didn't misbehave. We all had our duties like sweeping, dusting, setting or clearing the table, and washing dishes. And we were expected to help because she was Mama and we believed in her authority. With both parents, if they said we couldn't do something, we couldn't do it. I don't think I've ever thought in terms of being Mama's peer. No, she was Mama up on a pedestal. If she were in this room today, I'd still say "yes ma'am" and no "ma'am."

She would sit us down and tell us we couldn't be doing certain things and we were trusted to be good. We just never had any real hostility or anger demonstrated to us. She could be firm without angry words. Once one of my sisters said "damn," but she got her mouth washed out with Lava soap by Mama. I never heard Mama cuss and she wouldn't allow that language from us. You see, if we did something that needed disciplining, she'd tell Daddy when he came home and he'd break off a switch, take the leaves off, and switch our legs. That's about as harsh of a punishment as we got.

Mama was a good, loving woman. I keep coming back to love because we had so much of that. But loving doesn't necessarily mean putting your arms around and hugging. Loving is something you sense or feel and don't have to be told. It was just how she looked after us that was a sign of love. I knew she loved us because she sacrificed for us. She would deny herself things so she could provide for us. Now I don't want it to sound too dreary, because we were a happy family, but when I was in high school I had two skirts and some blouses and that was it. And when I was inducted into the National Honor Society in high school, Mother saw that I had a new dress. But she didn't have one so she didn't go.

Mary Lucinda Schermerhorn Dunlap

I never heard her say she wanted to do this or that without us. She always wanted to do things as a family. We always ate together and meals were simple. Daddy sat at the end of the table and always said the blessing, and my sisters and I would talk about what had happened that day. It was a happy time, a together time, and Mama always cared about what was going on in our lives.

And she cared about neighbors and friends. When someone was sick or died, Mama always took food and things to the family. And Mama was always easygoing about visitors. My Aunt Bessy would come to San Antonio for an Eastern Star meeting, and she'd appear at the door with a handful of people to stay with us. Mama would just have us pull mattresses off the beds and make pallets and it didn't bother her.

Mama had to stretch the money because Daddy was a machinist and we lived from paycheck to paycheck, but Mama could save money. Now we didn't realize we were poor because we were rich in love. In those days you could charge at the neighborhood grocery from payday to payday to keep things running, and somehow she always managed to pay the bill and also get us a little sack of candy. She was a good cook, but I've often said I didn't have an individual steak until after I was a student nurse and ordered a whole steak for myself at a restaurant. See Mama would buy round steak or a thicker steak and cut it in pieces. So we had plenty of food, but she made it go a long way because she was just so resourceful.

One time we were going on vacation, which was rare, but we had car trouble and it was going to take a lot of money to fix it, so Daddy told Mama we couldn't go. Well, Mama disappeared around the house, and when she came back she handed Daddy money she had pulled from her

Lillian Dunlap

brassiere. See, she had saved for the trip, which was typical of how she stretched things.

And Mama always supported me. When I went into nursing, I hadn't thought about going into the military. But when the war started I decided to go into the Army, and I spent two years in the Pacific. Mama was always sending me care packages, and I have a cedar chest full of pictures of me in uniform the first time I went home. If she had objected, she wouldn't have encouraged me and been so supportive. Anyway the day I entered, Mama saw me take my oath of office then she took me to my quarters and left her darling daughter there. I can remember that moment.

Mother always wore her little gloves when she went out. So when she died, we buried her in the pretty blue dress she had worn for her fiftieth wedding anniversary and those little white gloves. It just wouldn't have been Mama without those gloves.

Enchilada Sauce

>   3 Tbsp. shortening
>   3 tsp. flour
>   3 tsp. chili powder
>   Pinch of salt

Heat shortening and add remaining ingredients. After thoroughly mixed and browned, add 3 cups hot water. Cook until thick enough—may need more water. If hotter sauce is desired, add more chili powder. Pour over your favorite enchiladas and bake until heated through.

Spanish Rice

>   2 Tbsp. shortening
>   3 tsp. chili powder
>   1 small onion, chopped fine
>   Salt
>   1 large can tomatoes or tomato sauce, diluted
>   2 c. rice

Melt shortening; add rice and onion. When brown, add water. Mix chili powder in small amounts of water to dissolve, then add to rice mixture. Cover and cook slowly until rice is tender and all liquid has cooked out. Uncover about last 10 minutes to let the rice dry out.

Chili

>   2 lbs. ground meat
>   4 tsp. chili powder
>   3 tsp. flour
>   Pinch of salt

Mix last three ingredients into dry meat.

Melt 4 tablespoons shortening; add meat mixture and 1 medium onion, chopped. When well mixed, add 1 quart water and 1 small can tomato sauce. Cook until done, about 45 minutes. It helps the flavor to add a shake of catsup, Worcestershire sauce, and A-1 sauce. Garlic may be added if you like. Season to taste.

Chocolate Meringue Pie

1¾ c. sugar, divided (1¼ c. and ½ c.)
⅓ c. all-purpose flour
¼ c. cocoa
2 c. milk
4 large eggs, separated
2 Tbsp. butter or margarine, melted and cooled
1 baked 9" pastry shell
½ tsp. cream of tartar

Combine 1¼ cup sugar, flour, and cocoa in a heavy saucepan. Combine milk, egg yolks, and melted butter; beat, using a wire whisk, until well blended. Gradually add milk mixture to sugar mixture, stirring until smooth.

Cook chocolate mixture over medium heat, stirring constantly, until thick and bubbly (about 10 minutes). Spoon chocolate mixture into pastry shell. Set aside.

Beat egg whites and cream of tartar at high speed with an electric mixer until foamy. Gradually add remaining ½ cup sugar, 1 tablespoon at a time, beating until stiff peaks form and sugar dissolves (2-4 minutes). Spread meringue over top of pie.

Bake at 325 degrees for 25 minutes or until golden brown. Yields one 9-inch pie.

Lillian Dunlap

R etired Brigadier General Lillian Dunlap. As I only knew the name on paper, I must confess I had conjured up my own image of this military woman. After a knock on the front door, I prepared myself—standing almost at attention—but when the door flew back I smiled.

Before me stood Lillian Dunlap, who I guessed was barely over five feet tall and who had without a doubt one of the kindest faces I'd ever seen. She welcomed me in and immediately offered me a soft drink, cookies, and throw pillows to put behind my back for comfort. Without a second's hesitation, she launched into her mama stories, and I knew I'd best not dally since this tiny dynamo was off and running.

Lillian spoke tirelessly as she dovetailed information about her mama, herself, and the military. I listened as she spoke with candor about common sense and honor and integrity, then about all she attributed to having learned from her mama. She spoke of the love she has for her mama, and she spoke of the lessons in discipline her mama had given her.

Lillian Dunlap

After putting the puzzle pieces together, it made sense how Lillian Dunlap had risen to the ranks of brigadier general. She is a woman unafraid of duty and discipline, a woman whose judgments are based upon sound perceptions, and a woman of prudence and fair conscience. Born in San Antonio, Texas, in 1922, she has always returned to her hometown regardless of where her career has taken her. And that career has taken her all over—Texas, Colorado, Arizona, South Carolina, New Guinea, Okinawa, Washington, D.C., and Maryland.

Her higher education includes degrees from Santa Rosa Hospital School of Nursing and Incarnate Word College—both in San Antonio

—and Baylor University in Waco, Texas. And somewhere in between, Lillian joined the Army.

In 1942 she was commissioned as a 2nd lieutenant in the Army Nurse Corps and served on the staff of Brooke General Hospital at Fort Sam Houston, Texas. From 1943 through 1945 she was a staff nurse at the 59th Station Hospital in New Guinea. After returning stateside she was later promoted to assistant chief nurse then to chief nurse. From there her promotions included head nurse and chief nurse for the U.S. Army Medical Center in Okinawa, ending ultimately when she retired as brigadier general on September 1, 1975.

For her military service she has been honored with many awards: Distinguished Service Medal, Meritorious Service Medal, World War II Victory Medal, National Defense Service Medal with Oak Leaf Cluster, and the Philippine Liberation Medal with one battle star, to name a few.

But Lillian Dunlap's belief in service and discipline has led her in other directions also. Presently she is president of the board of directors for the Army Medical Department Museum Foundation, a museum she has worked tirelessly to bring to life. She also serves on the executive committee of the National Conference for Community and Justice, on the board of the Army Retirement Residence Foundation, and on the Nursing Advisory Council. The list of honors is also lengthy; however, a sampling includes: Who's Who in Government, Woman of the Year in Government, Texas Distinguished Citizen Award, San Antonio Women's Hall of Fame, and the Living Legacy Patriot Award by Women's International Center in California.

Perhaps it is this latest recognition which best describes Retired Brigadier General Lillian Dunlap, for she clearly can claim the title of a "living legacy patriot." And I bet Mama is proud.

Betty Sue Flowers

English professor, UT; author; business consultant

Betty Lou Lewis Marable

b. 1926

As a child I was aware that Mother smelled of musky and warm things—food, earth, spices. She would work outdoors and there would be this sense of all the things she'd done—the earth, just a lot of earth.

Baby Betty Sue Marable and mother, Betty Lou Lewis Marable

SOME TIME AGO MOTHER WROTE about her Depression era childhood, and if you read between the lines it's pretty amazing because her family is gleaning in the fields and selling squirrels for food. She recounts her mother as a hive of activity who had a hard life but describes her own childhood as being wonderful. Her family had no furniture, but to Mother that made it a great place for a party. She does not remember her story in terms of hardships, and she is still like that. She has this Scarlett O'Hara viewpoint that tomorrow is another day.

In her autobiography Mother describes how she and her sisters slept in the same bed and sang five-part harmony before going to sleep. Singing has just been a part of her life since she was young and in the Lewis Sisters trio. Had she not married they might have kept going like the Andrews Sisters.

I cannot think of Mother without hearing her singing around the house. Every Christmas for about fifteen years she'd be the spirit of Christmas Past in a church pageant, and I remember sitting in the dark holding candles and Mother's voice coming out over the entire church. Those were some of my favorite times. But when I took my son as a small child to those pageants, I also loved the feeling of being there with all the generations, Mother and me and her grandson, who associates Mother as the spirit of a Christmas angel, not as the spirit of Christmases past. Mother has beautiful white hair, and I remember watching her sing once and my sister whispering, "Isn't Mother an angel? She looks like an angel."

Baby Betty Sue Marable and mother, Betty Lou Lewis Marable

Mother's religious belief is one of relying on support systems bigger than we are, and my habit of relying on something that feels as if it's outside myself comes directly from her. I grew up feeling the universe has those supportive aspects. And Mother gave me a sense that life is good and if you trust it, it won't fail you. Now I think the way I work creatively is quite different from the way she works, but like her I have confidence ideas will come from out there.

During WW II my father had been a prisoner of war, and my grandmother had practically died she was so upset. So when he later went off to Korea, my grandmother believed he wouldn't be coming back. We were living with my grandmother then and Mother had just given birth to my sister, but the night Father left, Mother prayed and God told her he was coming back. So she had complete faith.

During the Gulf War, many young women from Killeen whose husbands went off to war would drive to Waco to talk with Mother. She has always been a mother figure to a lot of religious women, and she leaves a legacy of helping people. But they don't give awards for the kinds of things she does.

I think my mother's most influential trait for me is her ability to have lots of balls in the air at the same time and for it not to feel stressful. I can remember her in the kitchen with this old wringer-style tub on wash day. She'd lift out the clothes—which were too hot to hold—from the soapy water with big wooden spoons, put them into the rinse water, stick them through the wringer, then wring them out flat. I'd take out these hot, flat clothes and hang them on the line and watch the West Texas wind drive them straight out.

Mother, Betty Lou Lewis Marable and daughter, Betty Sue Flowers

When we were young I remember she'd ask us what shape we wanted her to make our pancakes for breakfast. So I'd tell her to make a toy truck or something really hard and she'd do it. I think about how usually when people are getting three kids ready for school and making breakfast they don't do festival-like things, but she made every day a special party. And on Friday nights we'd make popcorn balls or homemade taffy candy and have a family night sitting around and drinking hot chocolate, eating popcorn balls, and playing Parcheesi or Hearts.

And Mother would let me have sleepovers and she'd put us out in the backyard to camp out; I'd be telling stories and she'd be in the house cooking. Then she'd come out with goodies and leave, which is exactly what you want your mother to do when you're young. You know how sometimes children are ashamed of their mothers, well I don't ever remember feeling like that. She just had a good sense about how much to get involved, and I thought she was a perfect mother.

One thing Mother did through my teenage years was when I'd come home from school or a University Interscholastic League meet, she'd always wait up to hear about it. She just always listened and that is one of the sweetest things she gave to me. But now as an adult one of my fondest moments with Mother is whenever we visit we play double solitaire. We play these competitive games of double solitaire for hours and it's just us interacting. It's not a talking time, it's just a presence, a being there with our energy going full blast.

People always ask me how I do so much, and I have to stop and think. I know it's supposed to be hard, but it seems natural to me since I grew up with a mother who did far more than I did, although in a different domain. What I have inherited from her is this capacity for activity, and I use the word activity because it's the characteristic of being completely and usefully engaged. Mother designed two houses, landscaped gardens, upholstered furniture, made curtains, and was a Girl Scout troop leader, Sunday school teacher, and classroom mom. And she was active in church and civic things, yet nobody ever felt slighted because she could juggle a hundred things.

Mother has a sweet, innocent soul. I have never heard her say an unkind word about anyone, and I certainly have never heard her swear, my heavens, never. She is just sheer creative goodness, and to know she's there is a wonderful thing.

I asked Mother to give me this menu of recipes for a Sunday dinner because it is about her ability to juggle when you have to get three kids and yourself ready for Sunday school and get the Sunday lunch on the way.

Yeast Rolls

(Made on Saturday)

To 6 tablespoons of Crisco, add 1 teaspoon salt, ¼ cup of sugar, and a cup of boiling water. Set aside to cool. When cool, add 1 tablespoon of yeast softened in 2 tablespoons of warm water. Add 1 egg, beaten. Mix well. Add 3½ cups of flour, beating well after each cup. Knead on floured board until it can be formed into a soft ball. Place in greased dish. *(I take the ball of dough and wipe the bowl with it to get the top coated with oil.)* Cover and place in refrigerator until needed. It will be good for at least a week or more.

I often make cinnamon rolls with some of this dough. I roll it out thin, spread butter on it and cover with brown sugar, sprinkle cinnamon and chopped pecans. Roll up and slice into ½-inch thick rolls. Place in greased baking dish, let rise for at least 1½ hours at room temperature or while I'm at church. Bake in hot oven, 425 degrees, for 12 to 15 minutes.

Jell-O Salad

(Made on Saturday)

Mix 3 ounces cherry Jell-O with 1 cup of hot water. Stir until Jell-O is dissolved. Add juice from 1 can of pitted dark sweet cherries and about 1/4 cup sweet grape wine. Add cherries and pecans. Place in serving dish. Keep in refrigerator until serving time.

Banana Pudding

(Made on Saturday)

Combine ¼ cup sugar, 5 tablespoons flour or 3½ tablespoons cornstarch, and salt in the top of a double boiler; gradually add 2½ cups milk while stirring constantly. Cook over boiling water until thickened, stirring constantly. Cover and cook 15 minutes longer, stirring occasionally. Stir a little of the hot mixture into 3 egg yolks, beaten with ¼ cup sugar; stir into remaining mixture in double boiler and cook 2 minutes, stirring constantly. Remove, cool, and add 1 teaspoon vanilla extract or ½ teaspoon almond extract.

Meanwhile, cover bottom of casserole dish with crushed vanilla wafers and about 4 tablespoons of melted butter. Line edges with whole vanilla wafers. Cover crushed wafers with sliced bananas, and add half of cooled cream filling. Add more crushed wafers, more sliced bananas, and the remaining cream pudding. Cover with more wafers and meringue made with the 3 egg whites beaten with 6 tablespoons of sugar and ¼ teaspoon of vanilla extract.

Bake in slow oven at 300 degree for 30 minutes. Then remove and cool away from drafts. *Whipped cream can be used in place of meringue if so desired.*

Mashed Potatoes

(Peeled and cut into pieces and soaked in salted water over Saturday night; cooked in pressure cooker and mashed after church.)

Peel potatoes and slice, place in jars, cover with salted water, then cover with lids and place in refrigerator.

After church, drain and cook them in the pressure cooker for 10 minutes. Then mash them, add salt, milk, and butter for flavor.

Roast Beef

(Baking slowly while at church)

Wash roast and place in roasting pan, cover, and cook in 300-degree oven while at church. *(I usually put it in the oven around 8:30 or 9 A.M., depending on the size.)* It would be done by the time we got home, so I would slice it and make gravy from the liquid left in the baking dish.

Gravy

(Made after the roast has cooked)

Add cold water to about 2 or 3 tablespoons of flour to make a paste. Then add the paste to meat juices and stir over medium heat until thickened. Add water and salt depending on taste desired.

A Favorite Vegetable Dish

(Made after church)

Mix a package of frozen spinach with 1 can (drained) artichoke hearts, 1 small can (drained) sliced water chestnuts, 1 stick of butter or oleo (melted), and a 3-ounce package of cream cheese. Place in baking dish and bake until hot. Can be baked with the rolls. Toasted almonds can be added on top if so desired.

Betty Sue Marable Flowers

Near the end of a road with no outlet sits the home—nestled gently into the hillside—of Betty Sue Flowers and her family. Blended into a natural landscape that offers no hint of man's intrusion, the home seems a paradox—serene yet vibrant.

Betty Sue Flowers

Inside, the dishwasher's gurgling through mechanical cycles and the sweetness of pearl-colored roses in a vase atop the table provide a perfect sensory complement to the staccato chirping of a cardinal perched upon a bird feeder hanging from the house's eaves.

The petite and fair-skinned hostess, Betty Sue, has expressive eyes—prisms of an ageless soul—which appear like brush strokes upon the canvas of her face, a canvas of curiosity, humor, and compassion.

Betty Sue is a multifaceted career woman identified as a doctor of philosophy, poet, editor, business consultant, and award-winning professor of English. She holds a master of arts degree from the University of Texas in Austin and a doctorate of philosophy from the University of London; she has served as associate dean of graduate studies and director of the Plan II Honors Program at the University of Texas. Further testament to her educational achievements, this native Texan is a Piper Professor and a member of the Academy of Distinguished Teachers. She has penned numerous scholarly publications, a book entitled *Browning and Modern Tradition*, along with articles on Donald Barthelme, Adrienne Rich, and Christina Rossetti.

As a poet she has published two books—*Four Shields of Power* and *Extending the Shade*—along with poems in various journals. Her role as an editor is illustrated in the book *Daughters and Fathers*, as well as in four collaborative works with Bill Moyers—*Joseph Campbell and the Power of Myth*, *A World of Ideas*, *Healing and the Mind*, and *Genesis*.

As a consultant and businesswoman, Betty Sue has worked with Joseph Jaworski on the inner dimensions of leadership, has written and edited the global scenario for sustainable development sponsored by the World Business Council in Geneva, and is currently working on scenarios for the future of biotechnology. She also has served as moderator for executive seminars at the Aspen Institute for Humanistic Studies and as a consultant for NASA. And as for her visionary capacity, Betty Sue is a member of the vision team for the National Endowment for the Humanities and a Visiting Advisor to the Secretary of the Navy. She has also worked with Shell International in London to write global scenarios about the future of the world for the next thirty years.

When you become aware of all that can be listed on a résumé for Betty Sue Flowers, there is a realization that goes hand in hand with her accomplishments: This daughter shares her mother's trait of being able to juggle many things at once.

Randy Huke
artist; movie/TV set designer

Bertha Mae Kruger Smith

b. 1915

Mother's soul is huge and I don't even think her body can contain it. I think she has had a rich life as a woman and that everybody she touches is affected by her.

MY BROTHER DIED WHEN I WAS TWO so Mother really needed me as much as I needed her, and we bonded and became very close and have always remained close. There is just this connection between us and because of that it's like we've shared together in all the things that have happened to us. We are, I think you can say, really interwoven in that sense.

We've always been psychically connected. I'm one person that Mother trusts so she comes to me at times for help and advice, but I think that goes back to where we both can be honest about whatever we're going through. We have a very unusual mother and daughter relationship. My whole life, Mother has told me daily she loves me, and her voice is probably the most familiar thing to me. I think I probably heard it when I was in her womb. It is just total comfort, just total affection. We've always been very expressive of our love for each other. We are so in touch. I talk to her, to both parents, several times a day. So it's like we've had a

Randy with mother, Bert Kruger Smith, 1951

Bert Kruger as a young girl

dialogue that's gone on for at least fifty-two years, and I've always known I was terribly loved as it were.

I remember when I was sick as a child Mother would always bring me a tray with a flower, soup, ginger ale, and soda crackers. And I remember how when she put her hands on my forehead they felt smooth and cool. You know when you're sick with a fever how that feels to have this cool, comforting hand on your forehead. And I can conjure up that feeling at any point and it makes me feel safe.

I truly remember her hands being so graceful and elegant, so lady-like. My grandfather was a jeweler, but my grandmother did not like jewelry at all so he gave my mother lots of very unusual pieces of jewelry. And since she worked, I remember she always had on suits and beautiful jewelry and would let me dress up in her fancy dresses and play with her jewelry.

Another thing she did when I was young, which was really wonderful, was let me decorate my own room. I remember I was about four or five years old when we moved back to Austin and lived in this house where my new room had wallpaper with great big cabbage rose designs. I remember I would lie in bed and draw inside those roses. I think Mother knew but she never said a word. Then when I was ten or twelve it was time to redo the room so she let me pick out the color all by myself. For some reason we painted the ceiling the same color as the walls, and when we got through it looked like you were in a bottle of Pepto Bismol. But she wasn't judgmental; instead she suggested I do the accents in pink and black to kind of knock the pink down, so I did and loved it. But I had to live with that color until it was time to repaint the room, and when it was time I chose pale green paint. But you see she let me do what I wanted to the room.

I think Mother, both of my parents, gave me the freedom to find who I was. They would tell me things they thought I should do and offer suggestions, but then they gave me the freedom to figure it all out. Mother would give me her opinion, but she wasn't ever dogmatic, and no matter what she's been supportive of whatever I've done. We could always work on things together because she is such a facilitator and tries to help with whatever she can.

You know, what I thank her for the most is just always being there. We haven't been separated much, and I feel I can always call her up and tell her any problem I'm having and she will help me figure out a solution. She's always been giving to me not only emotionally but also with her time and attention. She's just, as my father has said, generous to a fault. She's such a fine lady and such a great example of a human being who deeply cares about her family and other people. There's just a softness in how she cares about and gives to others. I remember people calling her

Bert Kruger Smith

at all hours of the day with problems, and I was just amazed that she would always counsel them or get them help.

Whenever there was a meal or especially a big Jewish holiday, she and my dad would call the rabbi and ask if anybody needed a place to come and have a meal. So my parents always opened our home to others. That has been such a big part of who she is and she's always been that way.

If I had to choose some things Mother gave me it'd be integrity and honesty. You know as a kid it's a pretty terrible feeling not to be honest, so I learned pretty quickly she was right. Another thing I learned is I could trust her. If I told her something I didn't want her to say to anyone, she wouldn't say it. I always believed she would keep my trust, which is part of why I think we have a good relationship and sadly where I think some mothers and daughters grow apart.

She is very family oriented and definitely gave me the idea of family at all cost. I think she did a lot of the more traditional wife things, like when we moved back to Austin; my dad was in the real estate business and I can remember we always waited dinner for him no matter when he got home at night. That was just the way it was. We always waited for Dad to sit down to dinner, and she would put her day on the back burner and listen about his day. And at the dinner table we always talked about current events and had political discussions that were quite lively, and we laughed a lot.

But you know Mother also was a pioneer in the sense that she worked and had a career. It was an unusual thing for her to do at that time, and I think she had to be strong to forge ahead like that when a lot of women weren't working. She simply juggled so much, and I think she would have been called a supermom at that time.

It is interesting, but I think Mother's like a watercolor because I always imagine her in pastel colors. If I were to paint her it would probably be a mixed media, a collage, and it would probably bring in a lot of elements because I don't think she's simple in any way; I think she's just very layered.

I feel she is the perfect woman, the best mom a kid could have. I just feel so blessed not only to have known her but to have had her as my mom. It's been a great ride together, and we've had a lot of fun.

Mother gave me her love of cooking. That was something that my grand-mother loved, my mother loved, and I love, so that was passed down.

Lake Country Dip

1 bunch green onions, top and all, chopped
6 ripe tomatoes, chopped
2 4½-oz. cans chopped green chiles
2 4½-oz. cans chopped ripe olives
2 Tbsp. vinegar
4 Tbsp. oil
Garlic powder to taste
Tortilla chips

Combine onions, tomatoes, green chiles, and ripe olives. Toss with vinegar and oil. Add garlic powder to taste. Serve with tortilla chips and/or fajitas.

Mary Walsh's Potato Salad

8 medium to large red potatoes, diced
8 strips bacon or turkey bacon, cooked and crumbled
½ c. mayonnaise
Salt and pepper to taste

Cook potatoes for 15-20 minutes until done. When potatoes have cooled, add bacon pieces and toss with mayonnaise. Add salt and pepper to taste.

This potato salad recipe works because of its simplicity. Resist the urge to add other ingredients.

Randy Huke

To reach Randy Huke's home, I left the main road and snaked deeper and deeper into a canyon-like area. Homes built into hillsides—some small, others gargantuan—popped into view upon rounding each twist and turn in the road. The randomness in sizes was matched only by the randomness in styles, and overall it appeared this neighborhood had long ago left behind the idea that one must conform to the status quo. The air of daring in home designs prepared me to not be surprised when I reached the Huke home and found it too displayed a unique style, an artistic ambiance.

Bert Kruger Smith and daughter, Randy Huke

And it was not a surprise to find that the free spirit of Randy's homestead matched her winsome and expressive character. The buoyancy in Randy's voice belonged to a woman who apparently flourished in these surroundings. The multilevel house—which sits next to an art studio Randy shares with her husband—held an air of antiquity married to youthful originality. It was in the living room that Randy Huke, firmly grounded in her belief in good, spent two hours sharing her love for her mother. But long before the interview ended, I knew that Randy and her mother, Bert Kruger Smith, were kindred spirits in life.

Randy pursued and acquired a degree in the fine arts, specifically in painting, and has molded a long career that has allowed for personal creative expression. Most of her work has been in Austin, Texas, with the exception of one year spent in Oklahoma. Many of her efforts have involved teaching, first as an art instructor at St. Jude's Hospital for Emotionally Disturbed Adolescents, and from there at such sites as the Elisabet Ney Museum, the Kirby Hall School, St. Stephen's Episcopal School, the Laguna Gloria Art Museum, and Austin Community College.

However, Randy's artistic talents go beyond the classroom as she has exhibited her art in Colorado, New York, Missouri, Oklahoma, and Texas and has been involved with mural creations appearing in Oklahoma and Texas. And it has been her blessing to share many shows and mural work with her husband, John Huke, who is also an artist.

Randy, determined not to become static, branched out into new territory as a set decorator, buyer, and art director in the movie and television industry. Her set decoration work includes such feature films as *The Newton Boys*, *Lewis & Clark & George*, *The Faculty*, and *Where the Heart Is*. Her role as a buyer crosses back and forth from feature films—*Just Sue Me*, *The War at Home*, and *The Underneath*—to movies-of-the-week for television—*Locked Away*, *True Women* (miniseries), and *The People Next Door*. And as an art director her work ranges from *Body Snatchers* in 1992 to *Cadillac Ranch* in 1995.

While looking over Randy's accomplishments, it became evident that her mother indeed played a hand in destiny when she allowed the young pre-teen to lie in bed and paint inside the cabbage roses on her wallpaper, then paint her room—walls and ceiling—a Pepto Bismol pink. And with this freedom ingrained in her psyche, Randy Huke began the journey of sketching her life.

Luci Baines Johnson
chairman of the board, LBJ Holding Company

Claudia "Lady Bird" Taylor Johnson

b. 1912

What will I recall about Mother when the roll is called up yonder over on the other shore? Balance. An ability to give, an ability to take, an ability to love, an ability to be loved. And a passion, a lasting, life-long passion for learning and for service.

I LOOK AT MOTHER—who in her early childhood lost her own mother—and I see she had the sweetness of remembering a little but the reality of losing everything. Yet she blamed nothing on the fact that her mother had died, and she treasured what little she had. Mother is so stable and self-reliant, probably partly because death took her own mother. I often reflect, and I suspect my sister may as well, as to how she could be such an effective mother for her daughters when she didn't have the example of her own.

Lady Bird Johnson and baby Luci Johnson

I see how she managed to step into life and savor the complements of nature, and that's the model I want to be a part of. Her balance partly is from growing up in the East Texas piney woods where a love of nature was fostered and where she enjoyed and treasured those surroundings. Mother planted and nurtured with her hands and I saw that. What sustains her at eighty-seven years of age is the nature that excited and inspired her at age five. She saw drought come and kill and spring rains come and nurture, and she recognized that the sun would come up the next morning with faith and hard work. But she didn't put her emotional eggs in any single basket and was able to take what hand was dealt her and make the most of it. I realize that my mother recognized from the beginning it's not what happens to you so much as how you handle it.

Lady Bird Johnson and Luci Baines Johnson

And I've seen a tender expression of thought in her role as a wonderful wordsmith, a journalist, and a political observer, all of which sharpens one's vocabularies and skills to recognize the world around you in a keen way. Among the many things I thank her for, one is the gift of language. She has a passion to learn, and a day without something learned is a day wasted for Mother. She is a journalist by education, but you cannot be an effective journalist if you are not forever a curious person, and Mother is curious. If I had to say what gift I value most that came from my mother, from both parents, it is how she gave me a lifelong gift of curiosity. I think if a parent can give to their children a living example of the values they espouse, then there is no more precious gift.

My mother was gone a lot when I was a child, and I do not mean that in any judging way. She was a professional wife and knew that Lyndon Johnson needed a loving, wise, strong, present wife. And she was all of the above. She offered an extraordinary example, and when she was not there it was not because she was off being self-indulgent or because she was on some personal goal, it was because she was trying to do that which was in her goal of preserving her family.

And did I rant and rave and resent her being gone? You bet I did. And did I, like most children, vie for one parent over the other and try to pit them against each other? Yes. Did I put my mother through that? I am sorry and embarrassed, yes. But did I ever doubt that she loved me? Did I ever doubt that when she wasn't there it was because of any other reason than she was trying to make the world a better place for me and my sister? Never.

Lady Bird Johnson and Luci Johnson, graduation, St. Edward's University, Austin, Texas

With my mother there is a friendship, an example, a mentoring—all that she has afforded my sister and myself have been treasures beyond measure for us as adults. When a lot of mothers step back and go on to other things, Mother stepped forward, not in a hovering or demanding way, but in a loving and available presence, and that was a gift.

Mother has this wonderful inner radar that knows when somebody needs an uplift. I remember a time during the White House years when I was experiencing an adolescent crisis. My mother came and said she wanted to take me for a long weekend to a friend's country place where my parents had gone whenever life was stressful and they needed a getaway. Well, my mother just said we were going away for a few days, and I remember that dumbfounded me because she was the First Lady and I knew what her schedule was. But I underestimated her. I was having a crisis about my own sense of self-worth, and Mother showed me I was important enough to stop the world and get off. But she didn't just stop the world, she volunteered to stop the world, so it was anticipating my need and providing for it before I could even articulate it.

Luci Johnson, Lady Bird Johnson, and great-grandchild

A beautiful example of Mother being a protectress is when I went through my divorce, which grieved me and that I wanted to keep to my own heart. My former husband had left and I did not want to talk to anybody—other than my children—about it so I said nothing to Mother or another soul on earth. Now Mother has always enjoyed exercise and massage long before the rest of the world woke up to it, but massage was something she did; it certainly wasn't something I thought about. One day there was a knock on my door and it was my mother's masseuse; I told her Mother wasn't at my home. She told me she wasn't there for Mother, she was there for me, so when I looked perplexed, she said, "Your mother said you would understand." I just broke down into tears and said, "I do understand." You see, Mother wasn't about to invade and say, "I know you're hurting. I know you're troubled," but she was desperate to show she cared, so she sent some very feeling and loving hands to me.

Years later I saw Mother with another set of eyes. Our family was at the family ranch and my daughter asked me to bathe my granddaughter, Claudia. Now Claudia is one of these unbelievably placid babies who has been pure delight from the moment she was born, so I ran water in the bathtub and made sure it was not too hot or too cold. When I thought it was just right, I put Claudia—who I had bathed dozens of times—in the bathtub and she squealed to high heaven.

This was very much out of character, and I decided that maybe it was a strange bathtub in a strange environment. So I threw off my clothes and climbed into Mother's bathtub. But Claudia continued to squeal her little lungs out. I tried comforting her and realized nothing was working, so I got her out of the bath, wrapped her in a towel, and began to dry myself off.

Claudia kept squealing and Mother—at the age of eighty-six and with a fair amount of arthritis—came into her bathroom and asked, "What on earth is going on in here?" I explained the situation, and without saying a word, my mother—who is definitely more oriented towards adult mothering—leaned her cane against the wall, then she braced herself with her hands and walked herself down the wall onto her knees, crawled over to Claudia, sat down, and picked up this tiny, squealing baby, who instantly stopped crying. Mother had risked breaking a hip or something else, but she had heard this little girl screaming at the top of her lungs and knew she needed to help.

I looked at Mother and my jaw dropped, but I think the only other person more surprised than me was Mother. You could see this wonderful satisfaction and pride start at the top of her forehead and go all the way down to her toes as she rocked her great-granddaughter, who was now calm and silent, in her lap. I raced through the house, got my camera, and snapped a picture of the two of them, and when you understand the story behind that picture, it is an enormous victory. Mother had not let age or arthritis defeat her from answering the call of somebody she loved. So it was an extraordinary victory, an extraordinary moment.

Mother says life is ultimately divided into two categories—if only's and aren't we glads—and I think that sums it up. She is first and foremost always my mother, and I look at her as an influence, a loving, strong, grounded good presence in my life who chooses to be available to me to whatever degree I let her.

Custard is a "comfort food" for many Southern families. This version of baked custard has comforted generations of Johnsons.

Grapenut Pudding

3 c. scalded milk
4 beaten eggs
1 c. sugar
1 tsp. vanilla
½ c. Grapenuts cereal
½ tsp. nutmeg

Preheat oven to 350 degrees. Prepare hot water bath. Scald milk. Beat eggs. Add sugar to beaten eggs and stir well. Slowly add scalded milk to egg mixture, stirring constantly. Add vanilla and ¼ teaspoon nutmeg to custard mixture. Pour mixture into casserole dish. Finally add Grapenuts; sprinkle top with remaining ¼ teaspoon of nutmeg. Place custard into hot water bath. Bake until a knife comes out clean when placed into the center of the custard (approximately 1 hour).

Single recipe serves 4.

(This custard doubles easily, and our family nearly always wants it doubled!)

Mrs. Lyndon B. Johnson's Recipe for Pedernales River Chili

4 lbs. chili meat (coarsely ground round steak or well-trimmed chuck)
1 large onion, chopped
2 cloves garlic
1 tsp. ground oregano
1 tsp. comino seed
6 tsp. chili powder (or more, if needed)
1½ c. canned whole tomatoes
2-6 generous dashes liquid hot sauce
2 c. hot water
Salt to taste

Place meat, onion, and garlic in large, heavy pan or Dutch oven. Cook until light in color. Add oregano, comino seed, chili powder, tomatoes, hot pepper sauce, salt, and hot water. Bring to a boil, lower heat, and simmer for about 1 hour. Skim off fat during cooking.

Luci Baines Johnson

On the way to the interview with Luci Baines Johnson, I enjoyed the morning's blue sky and cool breeze as I took in the grand buildings rising up around me. I noted Austin's downtown energy offered a sense of excitement and ease, of formality and casualness. On the one hand, business people were deep in conversation with associates or were silently striding toward unseen destinations. While on the other, individuals unconcerned with deadlines strolled along or rode bicycles. And it was amid this study in contrasts I reached the Norwood Towers.

Crossing the building's lobby, I rode an elevator up several floors and stepped into the office of the LBJ Holding Company. Immediately I felt relaxed and before long understood that the surrounding atmosphere mirrored the poise and charm of Luci Baines Johnson. Once inside her office, we sat at a round table near plate glass windows overlooking the city below, and for two hours I enjoyed a world of Southern dignity and aplomb.

With composed ease, Luci honored her mother's legacy and spoke to a family heritage rich in heart and devotion. With respect she praised her mother's many contributions to society and family. Laughter and tears underwove Luci's reminiscings as her sensitive nature revealed innermost feelings about her mentor and friend—her mother.

Luci Baines Johnson

And after all was said and done, it was clear that Luci's personal achievements speak to her own capabilities and strengths. Luci is chairman of the board of the LBJ Holding Company, vice president of the Business Suites, and a member of the board of directors of LBJ Broadcasting.

She also serves the community professionally and publicly. Her roles include being a member of the board of directors of The Lady Bird Johnson Wildflower Center, the Children's Hospital Foundation of Austin, and the Texas public television station KLRU, and the honorary chairperson for the American Foundation of Vision Awareness.

Luci has received numerous awards recognizing her efforts and involvement: 1997 Top 25 Women-Owned Businesses by the *Austin Business Journal* and K-EYE TV Austin; the Distinguished Service Award from Georgetown University School of Nursing, 1996; Honorary Alumna of Vanderbilt University, 1993; Award of Recognition of Covenant House of Toronto, 1992; Honorary Member of Sigma Theta Tau, 1985; and "Special Friend" Award from the University of Texas in Austin, 1983.

And in addition her various community services have included: national president of the Volunteers for Vision, chairman of the Advisory Board of the University of Texas School of Nursing, and chairman of the Texas Affiliate Fundraising Drive for the American Heart Association.

In keeping with her strong character, she established the Luci Baines Johnson Centennial Professorship in Nursing at the University of Texas in Austin and received a degree in Communications from St. Edward's University in Austin at the age of fifty. Luci Baines Johnson indeed continues the legacy of achievements and service associated with the Johnson family.

Anne Trask Thomson Locker

b. 1910

*I think the greatest thing was my mom believed in me so much I don't have
anything that stops my creativity, that says that I can't make that happen.*

THIS IS A WONDERFUL MOMENT to put together all the things my mama meant to me and the impact she's had on my life. One thing I see is Mama working in a garden. We moved every year for the first ten years of my life, and the first thing she'd do was plant a garden. She always had her hands in the dirt, planting and being careful with what she had because we didn't have very much. She planted lots of pretty flowers no matter where we were, or she could take a little leaf and plant it in a pot and it would turn into some incredible thing because she tended it so well. She'd even take soil and put it in the oven to sterilize so she could use it again. She just loved nature.

Ernie and Anne Locker

Another image I have is of her extending herself to other people to make them feel special and welcomed. It might be that she'd take somebody's hand in her two hands and really look at them, or she might pat them on the back or something, but she was connecting with her hands. Mama and I always had a special appreciation for our relationship, and I know she had this wonderful delight and belief in me.

I always wanted to do everything under the sun, and when I'd tell her about stuff, she always encouraged and supported my ideas. We'd sit at the dining table and she'd listen to me and ask me about my thoughts. She never lectured, never moralized, never went on and on about something, so it actually was her reaction to me that made me believe I could do whatever I wanted to do.

One of the most wonderful things Mama did for me was give me self-esteem, not self-esteem like I think I'm perfect but an understanding that it's okay to feel good about myself. We had these things called TL's, and if Mama said she had a TL for me, it meant she had a compliment for me that someone had said and in return I'd have to give her a compliment. I grew up believing it's a good thing to tell other people how you feel about them, to tell them you love them, to tell them there's something special about them.

Anne Locker, Elf Louise Project, Christmas

Even though we didn't have a lot of money, Mama and I were into celebrating. If I had a whimsical idea, she'd immediately support me and we'd do it together. We'd spend hours searching for four leaf clovers, and I remember I had this sense that if we found a four leaf clover it was a sign that life was going to be wonderful and Dad would find a job. If we weren't looking for four leaf clovers, we were swinging and making up songs. There was this belief in the magic of life.

One Christmas we lived in this little bitty house where my brother and I shared a room. Well, Mama wouldn't let me in the kitchen for what seemed like an eternity. Unbeknownst to me, she was making me a dollhouse out of old apple crates that she covered with wallpaper samples, and furniture that she made out of blocks. She used felt for rugs and gathered material around a Band-Aid can to turn it into a dressing table. She even made a room with a plate glass window. It was incredible.

Louise Locker

But what I think is most interesting is that she had and then she didn't have. She came from this wealthy St. Louis family, but when we moved back to St. Louis after Dad lost a job, we lived in servants quarters. Then Mama decided to start a garden club. She called it the Grass Roots Garden Club, and it still exists. She handmade the club books and penned each one and planned the topic for each meeting. When I look back on this, it gives me goose bumps, it blows my mind that Mama had such grace and comfortableness with herself. She didn't have her own yard, and you can only imagine the yards of the people who joined the club. I'm in such awe that she could face the ups and downs in her life and always make the best of things.

She never complained. She was truly an optimist who had a lot of faith. If she even thought about complaining, she didn't give it much energy. She never rained on the parade, and she taught me through her faith to accept those things you can't change. She also taught me to have a gratitude for life. Because of her I have an intensified sense of how special life is, and if I get off track, I work on getting back on track to make the most of everything and not miss a moment.

She believed that magic and miracles and incredible things can happen. She believed in the potential goodness in people. She was always doing stuff for her church, like delivering flowers and visiting people, just quietly, never drawing attention to herself. She had about a hundred people's special days in a book, and she would always telephone in the mornings to tell somebody either happy birthday or happy anniversary. She did this, I want to say, without fail.

One year when we were in the middle of my Christmas project—the Elf Louise Project—somebody told Mama she didn't look well, but she said she was fine. Then without telling anyone Mama made a doctor's appointment. Ironically, the next morning when she was getting ready to go, she had a heart attack. I'm sure she was in pain, but in spite of that she put on her blue jeans, this belt with jingle bells on it, her plaid Christmas shirt, and her elf Christmas shirt that says "Elf Mama" on the back. When she got to the doctor's office, they immediately sent her to the hospital, and once they got her out of pain we sat and laughed until we cried. Then she said, "Louise, you've got things to do, go home and get your rest."

She died in the middle of the night. I had her funeral on Christmas Eve, one of the coldest days on record in San Antonio, but the church was packed with people. I had them play Christmas music before the service, and the church was filled with poinsettias; it was just incredible. And over and over people said to me, "I joined this church because your mom made me feel so welcome. She was the spark plug of hospitality at the church."

Even as grown up as I was, when she died I felt like an orphan. I felt like a little girl. My mom was this loving, precious light in the middle of this darkness.

Vegetable Casserole

> 3 1-lb. cans green beans, drained
> 2 4-oz. cans mushrooms, drained
> 2 5-oz. cans water chestnuts, drained and sliced
> 2 jars artichoke hearts, in dressing
> 1 c. condensed cream of mushroom soup
> ¼ c. melted butter

Mix. Drizzle butter over top. Bake at 350 degrees about 20 minutes or until bubbly hot.

Orange Cake

I yellow cake mix with pudding mix included
¼ lb. oleo
I c. orange juice
I tsp. grated orange
4 eggs

Bake at 350 degrees, 40 to 45 minutes.

Glaze for Orange Cake

¾ c. sugar
¼ c. water
¼ c. butter

Boil 5 minutes; add ½ cup orange juice; drizzle over cake.

Spanako Peata

2 pkg. frozen chopped spinach, thawed
3 eggs, beaten
4 Tbsp. flour
I lb. (2 c.) cottage cheese
½ lb. (2 c.) grated cheddar cheese
½ tsp. salt

Beat eggs and flour until smooth. Mix in rest of ingredients. Pour into well-greased 2-qt. casserole. Bake uncovered at 350 degrees for I hour.

Ham Casserole

I pkg. cooked macaroni and cheese
I c. fresh or canned mushrooms
I c. fresh or canned peas
I c. diced, cooked ham
½ c. milk
Butter
Bread crumbs
Dash of sherry wine

Combine the above ingredients using bread crumbs to cover, dotting them with butter, and pouring sherry on at end. Bake approximately 1 hour at 350 degrees.

Louise Locker

As I drove to the interview with Louise Locker, the Texas summer sun scorched the earth. However when San Antonio rose into view, gray clouds gathered overhead to cool the sweltering day. A good sign, I mused, as my spirits rose in direct proportion to the temperature's fall.

I maneuvered the truck through busy streets and parked alongside the curb in front of Louise's home. And from the minute I stepped into her elegantly comfortable home, it felt as though elfin sprites invisible to the human eye were sneaking peeks from behind furnishings and photographs. Then I noted Louise's eyes that danced with joy, and with but a few words exchanged I sensed a home filled with love and delight.

Louise Locker, born in St. Louis, Missouri, moved a lot until she was eleven years old and her family settled in San Antonio. Having a place to call home, Louise set in motion a course for life that would distinguish her as a woman who cares. While at Trinity University she helped others in the community when she founded the People to People Program, initiated a Big Brother, Big Sister Program, and recruited college students for various volunteer positions.

During those college years Louise began what would become her biggest social contribution. As a freshman, she gathered Christmas trees left in the dorms and put them in a vacant lot for people to take. The next year Louise began what is now known as the Elf Louise Project when she, along with her mother and a close

Louise Locker
Photo courtesy of Kirkwood Portrait Gallery, San Antonio, Texas

friend, provided Christmas gifts for the children of thirteen families.

From there the project has grown exponentially from thirteen families to twenty-five families, to one hundred families, and presently to ten thousand families. Over the course of time not one of the hundreds of volunteers has taken a penny for their efforts, reinforcing the spirit of spontaneity and caring that pervades the project.

Elf Louise does all of this on top of running a successful practice in psychotherapy. Although she has won numerous awards—the American Institute for Public Service Jefferson Award, the *San Antonio Light*'s Outstanding Woman, and the Good Samaritan Award from the Texas Emancipation Day Commission—this beautiful woman counts her son Chris as her most valued achievement.

At the end of my visit, mother and son shared in jokes, finished sentences for one another, and played duets on the grand piano in the living room. With innocent joy, Louise and her son filled their home with music and laughter. Suddenly it was clear that this woman has a gift, the gift of love and caring. And because she honors that gift, people are all the richer for it.

With the last sweet sound of the piano keys it was time for me to leave. As I bid Louise and her son good-bye, the skies opened up to a drenching rain. I ran to my truck and moments later, when I turned onto Interstate 35, one of the most prismatic rainbows I had ever seen graced the heavens.

Lydia Lum
journalist

Faye J. Lum

b. 1938

I have come to realize that my mother has her own sense of independence. Hers is in making decisions she is comfortable with and doing what she thinks she ought to do—then believing it is okay to make that decision. That is timely for me because she has played a large role in my coming to know this to be true.

A S FAR AS FROZEN MOMENTS, my mom and I did what you would call sort of a Joy Luck Club trip in 1996. Essentially we went overseas, and it was my mother's first time in thirty years to go back to Hong Kong to where, when she was seventeen years old, she had moved and lived for ten years as an adult.

Lydia Lum and mother, Faye J. Lum, Christmas 1973

On the trip we saw several people who were important to her, and that was interesting because it gave me a window into how she grew up, who was important to her, and what it meant to live in the Far East without really having the option of travel as we do here in the States. But to see all that through her was very eye opening for me. It was different to have her stories of being in that place put into context as opposed to simply hearing them.

I met my mother's great uncle, and I didn't even know we had one. We saw him almost every day, and she would say how she had been

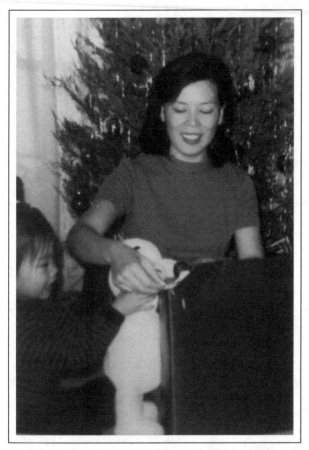

Lydia Lum and mother, Faye J. Lum

close to him and how he had done a lot for her. Then she would comment on how thin and frail he had become, and she would say she was glad she had come back because she didn't think he'd have much time left. It was her reconciling—because she hadn't seen him in thirty years—how she remembered a certain image of him.

I also met this man who she calls her teacher. Actually he was a professor of hers, and she was very close to his family. He had not had any daughters so my mom and her friend had become his surrogate daughters. What struck me was that for the first time I was actually seeing my mother interacting with somebody who was a father figure —her father had died before I was born. I saw her interact in a sense of deference but also with deep affection and admiration. She has always spoken very fondly of this man, so I felt honored and fortunate to have met him.

The trip was nostalgic of course, and to some degree she was reconciling how she remembered things and how they were now. She showed me her grandmother's apartment, and even though it turned out it was now run by some social service people, she stopped at the window to explain she was from the States and wanted to see the place where she had lived when she was in Hong Kong. We didn't stay long, but my mother showed me this tree outside a window and talked about remembering when she watered it. Then she remarked how she was shocked it was still there and had grown so big and was still healthy and how it was sweet that now it was a full tree one could climb.

But in a sense, it was that things were obviously so different from when she had lived there that caused her to experience many reactions of surprise. It was that my mother was seeing these changes and reconciling the reality of how things had changed, grown, died. I am glad I got to do that trip partly because there were a lot of emotions from joy to sadness, but also because it meant a lot to see my mother in those places and with those people. It was a true gift.

My mother has always taken an interest in what's going on within the family, so I guess one of her identities would be that of a caretaker. When somebody had an illness she would find out how she could help and lend support. Sometimes there would be a sick relative, and my mom would do something as simple as being the one who drove the car. She could just rise to the occasion and have very little hesitation to pick up the ball and organize things.

So I think I would say her soul is obviously very caring. I remember that when I was sick as a kid, my mother would rub Mentholatum on my chest, and I can remember how nice that felt. Or her caring could just be about something like fixing a cut. And this is an interesting example. I got into this tattoo stage one time, and I came home with a smiley face drawn in permanent marker on my hand. It would not come off with soap and water; it took nail polish remover to get it off. So it was highly unpleasant, and of course I got the lecture while she was removing it. But that is a different twist on how she cared enough to fix the problem, and she did it with patience.

Here's another picture I have of her in my mind. I am walking up the driveway to our house. I look through the parted curtains on the window leading into the kitchen, and I see my mother looking down at what she is doing. And that is a constant. Another thing I remember is that at certain times during the day or night she'd be washing dishes by hand, and that is another constant. Although that wasn't a time we would set aside, it was a time that would often occur. And I'd be sitting at the table doing homework, and you know it was like whenever Tim on *Home Improvement* goes outside and how it is never planned but there is Wilson at the fence. Well

Faye J. Lum and daughter, Lydia Lum

my mom is like Wilson and she is always there. It didn't strike me as being unusual, but those were moments that occurred millions of times.

Another thing I associate with my mom is her making Chinese dumplings. She never really talked much about learning to do the dumplings, but I'm sure it was something that was done in her home. My sister and I would try to learn almost as if it was a game, but I'm afraid we never succeeded. If you look at these dumplings, you'll notice how there is this intricacy in the twist you need to seal the dumpling so that there is no gap between the meat and the skin. And how she could sit there patiently and make a hundred of these then go onto something else is amazing to me. So I remember that about her hands, just their quickness, their agility in doing that. The whole memory is just a routine and it's very quiet, just like when I used to walk in the house after school.

My mom would not have minded had I chosen to go into law or medicine; however, she accepted and is supportive that I have chosen journalism as my profession. She has come to an understanding that this is something I want to do, to be able to understand someone's story enough that I can do it justice and tell it in a mass media sort of way. I'm pretty lucky.

Elbow Spaghetti

12 oz. large elbow macaroni, cooked
1 pkg. hot dogs, sliced - *we slice ours diagonally*
1 jar sliced mushrooms, drained
1 8-oz. can tomato soup
1 8-oz. can cream of mushroom soup

In Dutch oven or stock pot, heat cooking oil on low heat. Add hot dogs and stir fry until slightly browned. Add each can of soup, as well as two cans of water. Cook at low heat, stirring in mushrooms. When soup is blended and boiling slightly, add macaroni. Lower heat, stir. Ready to serve when blended.

Chicken Dressing

4 large stalks celery, chopped very fine
½ large onion, chopped very fine
1 pkg. Jimmy Dean sausage, regular
2 cans chicken broth
1 large loaf of white bread

Fry sausage in saucepan until completely cooked. Drain fat off completely and set sausage aside. Fry onions and celery in saucepan until just tender. Remove from heat and set aside. Bring chicken broth to a boil over medium heat. Remove from heat and let cool for a few minutes. Stir in sausage, onions, and celery. Add bread to broth mixture a few slices at a time while gently ripping up slices into small chunks. Stir mixture every five to six slices to incorporate the bread (bread will begin to soak up the broth). When all bread is mixed in, stir gently to be sure there is no excess broth; if there is, add a few more slices of bread. Spoon mixture into large oven-proof bowl or casserole dish. Place in oven for 10 to 15 minutes at 325 degrees until top of dressing is slightly dried out and crusty. Stir dressing before serving.

Dressing can also be baked with chicken in oven to add additional flavor.

Beef Stew

2-2½ lbs. oxtails
3-4 large potatoes, peeled and diced
4 medium carrots, chopped
¼ large onion, chopped
½ c. peas
2 medium tomatoes, peeled
Ginger (2 1-inch slices, peeled **or** ½ tsp. ground)

In large saucepan, fry oxtails briefly in a few teaspoons of oil over medium heat. When the meat has golden brown color on all sides, remove from saucepan and drain any oil/fat. In large pot, bring water to boil. When water is at full boil, place oxtails in pot. Be sure there is enough water to cover all the meat by at least one inch. Turn heat down to low, and simmer oxtails in water until tender, approximately 1½ to 2 hours. Check pot occasionally, stirring once or twice; add additional water should level drop too far. When meat is tender, remove oxtails and set aside.

Add chopped carrots to broth and simmer 5 to 10 minutes. Add diced potatoes next, simmer for a few minutes then add rest of ingredients. Bring heat back up to medium and bring stew to a boil. Add salt as needed. Add cornstarch paste to thicken (1 to 2 teaspoons with small amount of water). Add oxtails back to stew, turn down heat and simmer for additional 5 to 10 minutes. Serve over rice or noodles or alone with bread. (Serves 4 to 5 people.)

Lydia Lum

Looking into Lydia Lum's eyes, you see they speak of hope for the future. These portals of personality offer insight into a vibrant and adventuresome spirit. Her alert carriage and practical nature commix to present a woman with far-reaching goals. And so it is not surprising that by the end of the interview, Lydia Lum had reinforced my positive intuition about her character.

Lydia is a native Houstonian whose mother came to America from Hong Kong in 1967. Lydia—as a child and young adult—learned much of her vocabulary by reading the newspaper and watching television news, both of which led her to wonder what it would be like to report the news. She wondered how she could tell other people's stories through the written word while covering current events, and that led her into the field of journalism.

As a journalism graduate from the University of Texas in Austin, Lydia put her love of words to practice. She worked for the *Fort Worth Star-Telegram*, *Beaumont Enterprise*, and *Austin American-Statesman*, and most recently for the *Houston Chronicle*. Her assignments have included covering the Branch Davidian siege in Waco, Texas, as well as transition issues related to the 1997 handing over of Hong Kong from Britain to China. For her

Lydia Lum
Photo courtesy of David Paul Morris, 1999

expertise, Lydia has won awards from several Texas journalism groups and in 1999 was named Journalist of the Year by the Organization of Chinese Americans, a national civil rights group. All have been but stepping stones leading to her hiatus from the *Houston Chronicle* in order to travel and focus on a personal dream.

And that dream, her latest independent project, is tied to her Chinese heritage. Lydia believes everyone has a story to tell and knows she has the desire and talents to do so. Since 1998 she has been documenting the words and images of elderly Chinese detained and interrogated at Angel Island in San Francisco Bay prior to World War II. Of the two hundred thousand Chinese immigrants who faced attempted U.S. deportation under the Chinese exclusion laws, only a relatively small number remain alive, so time is of the essence.

Much of Lydia's Angel Island work has already been compiled into a traveling exhibition for museums, schools, and universities regionally and nationally. But today she is amassing more tales and photographs collected from her travels across the country to add to her ultimate plans of compiling the accumulated material into a book of oral histories.

Having watched her mother model a sense that it is okay to make decisions one is comfortable with, Lydia Lum is applying that very same lesson as she has chosen to take a leave from her newspaper job in order to become a historian of everyday heroes.

Judy Maggio
broadcast journalist; news co-anchor, KVUE-TV

Judy Maggio, mother Caroline, granddaughter Carly, 1991

Caroline Peterson Maggio

b. 1926

To me patience is one of Mother's biggest gifts. I remember maybe only once or twice in my entire childhood that she even raised her voice, and I don't think I've ever heard her be critical or judgmental about anybody. She's very sweet in almost a naive kind of way. It's so very refreshing.

I T'S HARD FOR ME TO PICK ONE IMAGE of her using her hands, but I can talk about several. The first one that comes to mind is writing. She writes beautiful letters, and even though she's not as mobile as she used to be because of her arthritis, she writes constantly. She always writes at the kitchen table, and I remember when I was growing up she would write these really long letters, so lots of times I'd give her stationery as a present.

Her junior year Mother was the editor for the *Houstonian*, the Sam Houston State University paper, and she graduated with an education

Caroline Maggio

degree. She probably would have gone into something like journalism but instead did some substitute teaching and ended up working as a dental hygienist. Then she became a homemaker. So you know in some ways I think her letter writing was kind of a release and an escape from the rigors of being a full-time mom. I mean, to be able to sit down for half an hour usually at night when things calmed down and be able to write what was going on, well that was a release for her.

Another image I have is of her sewing. She'd sit in her bedroom in the corner and sew by a window so it wasn't dark. That image sort of has a sense of comfort. She had her mother's old sewing machine, the kind you used your knee to operate, and she'd just sew. I can remember that. She made a lot of our clothes and uniforms—cheerleader and drill team uniforms—and I still have just about everything she made for me as an older child. I keep them in a chest.

The other image that is pretty visual in my mind is Mother playing hand games with little kids. She always taught church school to the preschoolers, and she is wonderful with three- and four-year-old children. So one of my big images is of her doing the itsy-bitsy spider and another hand game—I can't remember exactly how it goes, but it's something about a turtle and a pond and a fly. She can sit for hours with these preschoolers and entertain them with her very calm and soothing voice. When my daughter Carly was that age, Mom taught her all these little finger games. So I always think of her doing the

Judy Maggio and mother, Caroline Maggio, 1985

itsy-bitsy spider and other games.

You know, something I'd have to say about Mother is she's selfless. She has that selfless kind of love. Mother cared for her invalid mother for the last ten years of her life, so when I was a little girl and until I started school, we'd go over every single day and Mother would cook lunch for my grandmother. It was so much like a ritual of love. Grandmother was often in bed, and Mother would help her get in her wheelchair. I remember the house was creaky, you know from the wood floors, and there were stacks of books everywhere. Then there was the ritual of going to this old refrigerator and old-timey stove and preparing the food, and it was usually the same thing every day—a hamburger patty, carrots, and potatoes in the pressure cooker. I will see that the rest of my life, and it was just Mother's patience and perseverance, just the feeling that it was her job that made me know she didn't and still doesn't have a selfish bone in her body.

She's really a very inwardly strong person and a survivor. I think she could survive just about anything because she's dealt with lots of sadness in her life, and it doesn't seem to stress her out like it does most people. She felt the whole thing of caring for her mother was her duty, a daughter's duty, but I remember when my grandmother died, Mother simply said,

Vincent and Caroline Maggio, 1988

"Death has occurred." She even spoke at her own mother's funeral, which is something I could never do, but this just demonstrates that Mother has this inner core that's very strong.

And she has been strong like this for several friends of hers that were dying. It's just a very "angel on earth" kind of thing that she is supposed to take care of people, to just drop everything and do that. That's always been her selfless kind of role. I think I would say her spirit is goodness, just the very goodness of her soul and the ability to see that goodness in others. I mean she has these wonderful qualities, and I tell her what a good mother and what a wonderful role model she is.

She's talked about her inner strength coming from her Swedish heritage, and I tend to agree. She is a middle child with a sister who was mentally ill but a brilliant artist, and her parents were always dealing with this older daughter who had these problems. My mother had to be strong and take care of herself. Then she had this younger sibling who was very outgoing, so Mother was kind of caught in the middle. I think that's where some of this seriousness and strength came from.

I think her legacy would be about the giving of herself, especially through her church. She does a great many things, but one thing she's deeply involved in is a mission project in the rural part of Mississippi. She's made these contributions as part of her church to help better the lives of underprivileged people. She's the embodiment of what a religious person

Judy Maggio (middle) with father and mother, Vincent and Caroline Maggio

should be, what all the faiths teach, that you give of yourself to others, that you want a peaceful world.

Both of my parents are leftover hippies and peace activists. They have been very involved in peace efforts and are part of several councils and groups in Houston whose main goals are to promote world peace. As a matter of fact, in 1991 Mother and Dad received a Lifetime Achievement Award from the Houston Peace Network. Mother has managed to achieve this goodness, this kindness that I talked about, and it just comes naturally for her. It's an amazing thing.

Mother's voice is one of comfort. It's always soft, never loud, and just comforting and calm. There's a certain calming presence there. I still want my mother when I'm sick. I envision her coming to me and giving me soup or patting me on the back.

My mother is a very simple person, including her cooking. It was a big joke with our family that everything was cooked in a pressure cooker. But these recipes were things she made a lot, and they're all baking recipes. Whenever we'd have a function to go to when I was young, like a church activity, I always remember her making this orange date cake. Then something we had every Sunday morning were these wheat germ raisin muffins. And now, as we've gotten older, she always brings applesauce cake when my parents come to visit. These recipes are all simple and healthy.

Orange Date Cake

1 c. butter
2 c. sugar
4 eggs

Combine 2 tablespoons grated orange rind and 1 teaspoon vanilla. Add to above and blend. Sift and add to creamed mixture 3½ cups flour, 1 teaspoon soda, and ½ teaspoon salt alternately with 1½ cup buttermilk. Fold into cake mixture:

1 c. snipped dates
1 c. chopped pecans
(both coated with ½ c. flour)

Bake in greased tube pan for 1⅓ hours at 325 degrees. When done, pour over hot cake a glaze of:

1½ c. sugar
1 c. grated orange rind
1 c. orange juice

Raisin Muffins

1 c. raisins combined with ⅓ c. sugar
1 c. sifted flour
2 tsp. baking powder
½ c. sugar
¾ c. wheat germ
¼ c. butter
1 egg, beaten
½ c. milk

Melt butter and let cool. Combine raisins and ⅓ cup sugar. Sift dry ingredients together. Stir in wheat germ. Combine melted butter with egg and milk. Add all at once to dry ingredients, stirring until just moistened. Mixture should not be smooth. Fold in raisins. Spoon batter into muffin cups. Bake at 400 degrees for 20 to 25 minutes. Yields: 12 large muffins.

Applesauce Cake

2 c. sifted flour
1 c. sugar (or less)
1 tsp. cinnamon
½ tsp. nutmeg
2 tsp. baking soda
1 c. raisins
1 c. nuts
½ c. melted butter
2 c. (1 lb. can) applesauce
Grated lemon peel

Sift together dry ingredients. Stir in raisins and nuts. Add other ingredients and beat until well blended. Pour into greased pan 9 x 9 x 2 or 11¾ x 7½ x 2. Bake 45 to 50 minutes at 350 degrees. Cool. If iced, powdered sugar, butter, and lemon juice is suggested.

Judy Maggio

If you have the good fortune to find yourself in the company of Judy Maggio, you cannot help but feel refreshed and invigorated. She has a spirit of joy that manifests itself through her smiles, eyes, and personality. Laughter and tears come easily for Judy as she is a woman of emotion who is in tune with life. She listens as intently as she talks, and when you consider all of these aspects of her character, it is no surprise that she has chosen broadcast journalism as her profession.

The course that led to her career began when she was a student at Milby High School in Houston, Texas. Her successful involvement and performances in debate, speech, and poetry reading caused her high school speech coach, Ed Thompson, to urge her to consider broadcast journalism for a career.

Taking Mr. Thompson's advice, Judy attended the University of Texas in Austin and acquired a journalism degree in 1981. However she claims her big break in the field occurred before she graduated when Carole Kneeland, a Dallas reporter, came to the university seeking interns for the Austin bureau of a Dallas television station. After interviewing several candidates, one of the positions was awarded to Judy, and to this day Judy credits Ms. Kneeland with teaching her the necessary ropes for achieving success in the industry.

Judy Maggio
Photo courtesy of Mike Wenglar Photography

Judy's professional career began in 1981 as a general assignments and medical reporter for KVUE-TV, Channel 24 in Austin. While carrying out those roles, she was named weekend anchor for the station, a position she held from 1984 until April of 1985 at which time she was given the title of weekday co-anchor for the six o'clock and ten o'clock evening news. Along with that role, she also became managing editor for the news in 1995.

For Judy it is simple. She explains that her passion is people. That she is intrigued by people and who they are, and she loves to learn about them, their lives, and how they got to be who they are.

Over the years Judy has received numerous awards which include: Austin Communicator of the Year, 1997; *Austin Chronicle*, Best of Austin, Best Anchor award, 1994-1997; Best of Gannett, Best Anchor Reporting, 1995; Best in U.S. by U.P.I., 1987 and 1990; the Texas Veterinary Medical Association Media award for a co-anchored newscast, 1989; the American Cancer Society Media award, 1987 and 1988; and the Texas Hospital Association Media award in 1988.

Judy Maggio is considered one of the most familiar faces on television in Central Texas. And once you have been around her and experienced the music of her voice—a voice that resonates with a love for life—you will never forget her.

Laura Martinez-McIntosh
attorney; educator

Laura Martinez-McIntosh and Maria Martinez

Maria Luisa Renteria Martinez

b. 1946

I wouldn't say the greatest gift my mother has given me is anything material. When I was growing up she used to always say it is what you know and what you think that another person can never steal from you. So it was not feeling like the physical things were so important, but that it was more important what you have inside.

149

AT THE CORE OF MY MOTHER'S IDENTITY is that she is a survivor, a leader. As the oldest sibling in her family, she had to step into a role of being like a mom, so I think from that she acquired the qualities that made it possible for her to be such a good leader. She is the leader who has always gotten everyone together and kept the family communicating with each other, and she's still very much the diplomat with her brothers and sisters.

But if I had to get a mental snapshot of my mom, it would probably be her in the kitchen in this very traditional role, methodically beginning her preparation for the whole day. In the morning it would be a picture of her with curlers in her hair, and she would be in the kitchen making coffee for my father and putting together his lunch for work. Then she'd get his clothes ready and make sure he had his briefcase, and at the same time she managed to feed and take care of us kids. After he would leave, she'd put on her makeup and fix her hair, then start cooking to make sure she'd have

Maria Martinez

dinner ready by the time my father returned. By the afternoon she was beautiful, and what she taught me through this daily routine was that she did those things for my father because she loved him.

Most definitely a way she showed her love was through the food she prepared. I mean, I knew she loved us because she took the time to do all that cooking, and I think there is something to the idea of making food with love. You have to have patience and you have to care what it's going to taste like. I just remember Mother making tortillas. She'd knead the dough, store it, and let it sit, then she'd take it out and roll it out. And it was just the smells and watching her flip it over then offer it with her hands to me. And of course if I ate it, that was a sign that I liked her food, so the emotion I get with Mother's food is love.

My mom and dad are both strong believers in sharing meals and food. There's a lot of effort put into them, and you realize it's more than just food as a source of nutrition, but rather it's food as a celebration. And when I think of my mom cooking, I think of how it is a big part of who she is, this woman who makes great meals for those she loves.

Now this is an interesting snapshot of my mother in the kitchen. When she was growing up she thought it was sad that her family didn't celebrate birthdays, so when she reached an age where she could do something about it, she started baking birthday cakes and planning the celebrations. I think that is why her cakes are such an important part of her because it is how she can show the people she loves how much she cares about them.

Still to this day she makes sure her brothers and other members of her family have cakes on their birthdays. She doesn't forget. She makes sure it's on the calendar, and she even delivers it. She makes cakes for weddings too—that is her gift. So you can see why on Mother's Day she doesn't just get gifts from us. She's just very kind to people and extremely giving, not only in a physical sense but also in an emotional sense. I know she is giving these gifts, these cakes, but she's also really giving of herself. Her spirit is kindness.

My mother, actually both of my parents, always made sure that we kids had what we needed. If you look at our house you can see it was tiny when we were growing up, and they have added on over the years. But if you look at which rooms were completed first, you see that their room was the last. They put us first because they didn't feel like they needed a whole lot, and my mom truly cared about us having the best.

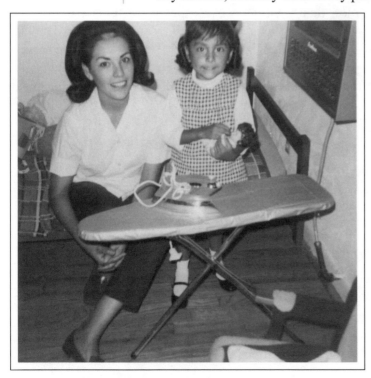

Maria and Laura Martinez

She was very demanding in schoolwork and pushed us to excel. She had grown up in a home where they only spoke Spanish, and she had gone to a school where the children weren't allowed to speak anything but English. So she had bad memories of being in school and not being able even to ask to go to the bathroom and of going home and not being encouraged to do well in school. As a result, she wanted to make sure we did well. She wanted us to make the best grades possible, and I remember when I was little she would buy a spelling bee book every year. In the evening she and I would go through it and she would recite the words and I'd have to spell them, and I remember just getting so tired of doing that. But I won one of the contests in our school and went on to represent our school at the citywide spelling bee. Once I did that she had that same expectation every year. I can hear her saying, "You can do it. You can win. You can be the smartest kid in your class." And when you are sixteen and seeing you can do all these things—make the grades, win the scholarships, be salutatorian—then you see what your mother is saying is really true and you start to believe.

Growing up my mother became my best friend. I could tell her anything and to this day I still can. She is just someone I can rely on, and since I've been gone from home—first for college and now in my job—it has never failed that there was a regular time we knew we were supposed to call each other on the phone. When I was in the university it was on Saturday mornings, but since I've had my job and gotten married, we talk on Sundays.

Over the years I have saved all of her letters. They're in this huge box, and it's a history more than anything because they weren't just letters to say I love you. They were about what was happening in the family. The last time I went home I brought them back with me. But still when I see one, I have this mixed sense of excitement and nostalgia. They always make me want to tell her thanks for being there for me and for her encouragement and for her loving me. For her just being a loving and accepting mother who let me be who I am.

My mother's legacy is that she is leaving memories for lots of people she took care of, and I think they are going to pass those memories down in the form of stories. And she'll be remembered for many things—her kindness, her caring, and for being the woman who made the cakes.

Flour Tortillas

4 c. flour
2 tsp. salt
1 tsp. baking powder
½ c. shortening
1 c. hot water

Mix dry ingredients; work in shortening and water. Knead dough until it doesn't feel sticky; add a little flour if needed. Let it sit for a couple of hours then make egg-sized balls and let them sit for a while in a plastic covered bowl. Flour a board and roll dough balls to about 8 inch. Bake on a hot griddle and turn tortilla over. Keep in a tortilla holder (foam bowl with lid). When they have cooled enough, keep them in a plastic bag in the fridge. This recipe makes about 3½ to 4 dozen tortillas.

Sauce for Enchiladas or Mole

Brown 2 cups flour in cast iron skillet (be careful not to burn) and let cool. Add 1 ounce chili powder (Gebhardt). Stir together and add about 4 cups chicken broth. Over medium heat, keep stirring until you get it as thick or thin as needed. Also add salt to taste.

For mole: Have chicken already cooked. Put chicken in hot sauce and it is ready to serve.

For enchiladas: After dipping corn tortilla in hot grease, dip in sauce and they are ready for filling.

Cream Puffs

1 c. water
1 stick margarine
1 c. flour
4 eggs

Bring water to a boil in a saucepan. Add margarine and melt then add flour. Stir until mixture makes a ball that will not separate. Remove from heat and add eggs one at a time, mixing well. Drop by spoonful on greased cookie sheet. Bake in hot oven at 450 degrees for 15 minutes then at 325 degrees for 20 minutes. Allow to cool and fill with vanilla pudding. Sprinkle with powdered sugar. Makes 1 dozen.

Laura Martinez-McIntosh

All too often society gauges a person's worth by outward and material items—the type of car they drive, the size of house they own, the style of clothes they wear. But these items are simply on loan, temporary toys at best, and can be lost in the blink of an eye without much regard to the owner. On the flip side, there are things that even though they cannot be held in the palm of a hand are everlasting gifts which constitute the true value and character of a human being. Laura Martinez-McIntosh—a petite, soft-spoken young woman—refers to such intangible gifts as the life lessons passed along to her from her mother, Maria Luisa Martinez.

Laura believes the greatest treasures she has received from the matriarch in her life include the beliefs that it is more important what you have inside than what you display on the outside, and it is what you do for others that enriches your soul and delineates your legacy.

Laura Martinez-McIntosh

Taking these lessons to heart, Laura is sculpting a life where she perpetuates those "Mother truths." After receiving a bachelor of arts degree in psychology from the University of Texas in Austin, Laura listened intently to an inner calling and made a decision to work in the area of justice. The result of that decision manifested itself when she worked toward and received her Doctor of Jurisprudence degree from the University of Houston Law Center in 1990.

Licensed to practice law in both Texas and the District of Columbia, she accepted her first job as a staff attorney at AYUDA Clinica Legal Latina, a nonprofit organization in the District of Columbia that represents immigrant women in obtaining protective orders. During that time she also trained D.C. police officers on mandatory arrest and how to respond to domestic violence calls.

Currently she is a staff attorney with Legal Aid of Central Texas in the Family Law division and a part-time adjunct professor at the University of Texas School of Law in the Domestic Violence Clinic. Laura assists survivors of domestic violence in obtaining protective order, custody, child support, and divorce. She provides training in Texas on various issues with the Texas Council on Family Violence and is a resource for immigrant and refugee survivors through the National Domestic Violence Hotline.

For her skills, Laura was chosen to participate in a workgroup on urban health issues to identify and explore the central issues surrounding the impact of violence on the health care of substance-abusing women and their families in at-risk, primarily urban environments. She was also a member of the review panel on Domestic Violence Against Women with the Maternal and Child Health Bureau of the Department of Health and Human Services.

And so it is that this advocate for the people is applying the life lessons she learned so obviously well from her mother. Electing to forego the material, Laura Martinez-McIntosh is securing a legacy built on doing for others.

Angela Shelf Medearis

vice-president, Diva Productions; author

Angeline Davis Shelf

b. 1932

My mom showed me about taking care of your family, cooking a good meal, keeping your man happy, and doing something for yourself. She showed me the joy in doing simple, common everyday things if they make someone happy, and those were all gifts, but I think my favorite gift is one I can't pull out and show you—the love of telling stories.

H ER MOTHER AND FATHER and her family have always been the most important and most influential people in my mom's life. They lived on a farm and were pretty close knit, and today our family is important to all of us. My closest friends are my siblings. We shared the bedroom, the clothes, and have always stuck together and looked out for each other.

Mother, Angeline Shelf, daughter, Angela Medearis

Mom has a big thing about taking care of your family and has always stressed that "charity begins at home." That has been good in my life because the way I gauge people is in how they treat others, and I have learned that is the true measure of a person.

Both parents reared us well, and together they gave us the tools we needed to excel. I don't remember either parent ever saying, "You can't do that. You're not capable or smart enough to do that." They never said those things, so we thought we could do anything because they raised us with enough self-assurance that when we did hit the slings and arrows we just came out on level ground and were fine.

You know, all I wanted was to be left alone so I could read, and Mom let me do that. Sometimes she'd try to drag me out to get some fresh air, but she was good about letting me be who I am. She just let us kids be what we were and never compared us to each other. I remember she'd say to me, "You are my favorite child," but, and this is funny, I know she told us all we were her favorite child. She just knew how to give us what we needed, and that's a real talent because sometimes, when we'd be so wrapped up in things, she'd know it was time to put a little love on us and make things better.

Through her I realized that being close to God didn't have to do with how much you went to church, it was more in what you know to be right and trying to live by that.

Mom raised us in a way that we knew we weren't handicapped or crippled even though there is a racist society and we are going to deal with a lot of crazy stuff. She taught us not to blame failures on this fact or that person. Instead she raised us to think that if this door's closed, then drag up a trash can because there's a window or a chimney, so just get in there and do it. The front door is only one option.

I was fortunate because my dad was there to keep me on the straight and narrow and my mom was there to shepherd and guide me. Most of our lives we were moving, and there wouldn't be any family around to watch us kids, so she'd send us to church on Sundays. Now it didn't matter which church—Catholic, Lutheran, Methodist, Baptist—it was just whatever church was within walking distance. So we'd be off trying to figure out which religion we were at the time, and she'd be at home putting on dinner and spending private time with my dad.

She has a divine spirit, she really does. Through her I realized that being close to God didn't have to do with how much you went to church, it was more in what you know to be right and trying to live by that. She is just a peaceful, serene person with a deep belief in God that has nothing to do with sitting up in the building. She just knows the ins and outs from living, and she believes that if you live right and learn from your mistakes, then by the time you get to a certain age you're rocking along.

Mom always says, "You have to crawl before you can walk." After I got married and we were having a hard time, we'd visit her and she'd pack sacks of groceries for us to take home, and she'd say, "It's going to work. You just keep on, it's going to work." She simply feels you're not going to start off at the top, that you might crawl for a time but you're going to get up and walk, and the struggle is just part of the process.

From watching her I found out how important it is to have something that's your own, that even though you're a wife and a mother you still need to have an outlet. It's interesting that women often consider it selfish to take time to find what it is they enjoy, but by watching my mother do her art projects I learned it was okay. I remember her in the kitchen when she was creating and it'd be late at night and stone quiet because everybody else was asleep, but she'd be working on her projects. And through those projects she taught me what a joy there is in making a home nice.

If I were to put my mom up on a pedestal what would she be? I always get those images of a geisha girl. You know how serene and graceful they are and how you're not quite sure what's going on in their minds even though you know there's a lot going on. They just keep their own counsel and make sure everybody's comfortable and taken care of. So my mom has a geisha kind of personality.

A visit to my mother's garden is a kind of poetry in itself. Every green, leafy row has an earthy, poetic pentameter. The rich warm black earth has a wonderful smell, like a vegetable casserole baked under a blazing sun. I like to sit between the rows while she picks the greens and listen to her voice drift over to me as I close my eyes and enjoy the sun. I could have anything I want from my mother's garden, but I know my mother wants me to have what she loves and enjoys the most, greens.

Greens and Okra

> 2 c. chopped ham pieces
> 3 c. water
> 4 bunches collard greens
> ½ Tbsp. salt
> ½ tsp. sugar
> 1 or 2 dried cayenne pepper pods to taste
> 8 to 12 small baby okras, stemmed

In a heavy pot or Dutch oven, simmer ham in water until tender and fat dissolves, 15 to 20 minutes.

Cut the tough stems and yellow leaves from greens and discard. Gently rub leaves with fingers under warm running water. Cut greens into large pieces. Let leaves soak in warm, salted water for 10 minutes. Rinse with cool water and drain in a colander.

Add salt, sugar, and peppers to ham, then add greens. Stir every 15 minutes until greens are wilted but not quite tender, about 30 to 45 minutes. Layer okra on top of greens. Cover and continue cooking greens and okra for 10 to 20 minutes or until tender, stirring occasionally and adding hot water as needed to prevent greens from sticking. Makes 6 to 8 servings.

Pineapple Upside Down Cake

Topping:
> 4 Tbsp. butter or margarine
> ½ c. firmly packed brown sugar
> 1 (30 oz.) can pineapple slices, drained
> 10 maraschino cherries

Cake Batter:
> 2 c. cake flour
> 2 tsp. baking powder

¼ tsp. salt
¼ c. vegetable shortening
I c. sugar
I large egg, beaten
I tsp. vanilla
¾ c. milk

To make topping:

Grease an I I x I4-inch pan with I tablespoon of butter. Sprinkle brown sugar in the pan. Place a layer of pineapple slices on top of sugar. Place a cherry in center of each slice. Dot remaining butter in and around pineapple slices.

To make cake batter:

Sift together flour, baking powder, and salt in a medium bowl. Cream shortening in large bowl, gradually add sugar, and beat until fluffy. Add egg and vanilla and mix well. Alternately add flour mixture and milk—in small amounts—and stir until batter is smooth.

Pour batter over fruit topping. Bake at 350 degrees for 50 to 60 minutes until cake is brown on top and a toothpick inserted in the cake center comes out clean. Cool cake in the pan 5 to 8 minutes. Place a serving platter on top of cake pan and turn upside down to release cake onto platter.

Cabbage Smothered with Bacon

3 slices bacon, chopped
I small head cabbage, washed and shredded
I large green bell pepper, sliced
I large yellow onion, sliced
I large tomato, peeled and chopped
3 stalks celery, cut diagonally into thin slices

Fry bacon until crisp in large skillet or Dutch oven. Remove bacon and set aside, reserving bacon drippings in the pan as they will add flavor and moisture to cabbage. Add cabbage, bell pepper, onion, tomato, and celery to pan. Raise heat to high and fry vegetables, stirring constantly for 5 to 8 minutes or until vegetables are crisp-tender. Cover pan, reduce heat, and simmer vegetables for another 5 minutes. Crumble bacon and sprinkle over vegetables. Yield: 6 servings

Angela Shelf Medearis

Minutes into the interview with Angela Shelf Medearis, the image of a dynamic river rushed into my thoughts as Angela leapt into the moment and her unbounded energy swept me along its swift course. Surrounded by floor-to-ceiling bookcases overflowing with books and mementos, Ms. Medearis first talked about her move to Austin in 1975, then her thirteen-year stint as a secretary.

Angela Shelf Medearis

She mused about the clash with bosses in 1987 which sent her on a new career course in writing. She recalled how "at first it felt odd to sit at home and write" because it was so foreign to her to think she could "make a living at it." And a good living she has made through her craft as a wordsmith.

She served briefly as a publicist for the now defunct Texas Monthly Press, then became a freelance writer for *Crisis*, a magazine of the N.A.A. C.P., which allowed her to focus on black contributions to art and stories based in Texas that spoke to African Americans. However during her freelance writing, Angela confesses she found herself thinking about the stories and books—almost devoid of black children, men, and women—that she had read so feverishly as a child. After examining the existing market, Angela decided upon a personal journey to change the direction of children's literature, and she launched a career in writing children's books that reflect the African American heritage and life.

Her first work—literally a gift of story from her mother—was *Picking Peas for a Penny*, published in 1990 by State House Press of Austin. Its success led to a reprint by Scholastic Incorporated, one of the nation's major publishers of children's books. From that point, Angela's writing legacy leaped forward as contracts with MacMillan, Holt & Co., Holiday House, Penguin, and other publishers soon followed. To date, Angela has produced over seventy books with black characters or themes and is credited with close to three million copies of works in print. She is considered one of Texas's most prolific and most successful authors of children's literature.

Enmeshed with writing her children's books, Angela also created a program called Book Boosters to provide tutoring programs for students in area public schools. And she pursued the writing of cookbooks—*The African-American Kitchen, The Kwanzaa Celebration Cookbook,* and *Ideas for Entertaining from the African-American Kitchen.*

And if that is not enough to make the average person gasp for breath, Angela's recent business venture places her in the role of vice president of Diva Productions, a film, television, and theatrical production company designed to create and produce concepts, scripts, and videos that provide a view and a voice of African American life seldom explored and heard in those mediums. Her narrative documentary *Always a Bridesmaid* landed Angela as one of twelve finalists for the Aperture 1999 Short Film Grant. She also received recognition as a semi-finalist in the Chesterfield Screenplay Writing Competition for her screenplay *Kountry.*

Days after the interview, I picked up a copy of *Picking Peas for a Penny*—the work that propelled Angela on her literary path, and as I read, the lingering bell-like tones of Angela's voice played in my mind. Once I finished, I sent my thoughts back to two lines, "Plenty work to be done, In a field full of peas under the morning sun." I heard the underlying perseverance behind those words and sensed the spirit and strength that captures the natures of both Angeline Davis Shelf and her daughter, Angela Shelf Medearis.

Kitty Argersinger Mellenbruch

rancher; educator

Flo Rae Anderson Argersinger

b. 1927

I feel that when you look back on your life, the only person who ever honestly loves you and accepts you no matter what is your mother. She overlooks all of your faults, your flaws, the things you say. She loves you unconditionally, and that's the way I feel about Mom.

THERE'S NO ONE who will love or look out for me like Mom does. There's no doubt she'd do anything for me to the extent of suffering herself and that she would give of herself and never complain. She'd just do it, period.

I think for someone who grew up during the Depression, she had an interesting life. Her father worked for the Santa Fe Railroad and ran a depot in Matagorda. Her mother stayed at home so they didn't have a lot of money. My mother's brother, when young, was sickly so she had to do more of the chores, but she wasn't afraid of work. One story she talks about is when she was nine or ten years old, her family didn't have the money for her to go to camp. So Mom would braid the hair of two girls who lived across the street, and she would gut and gill fish in order to earn extra money for camp.

When she was fifteen or sixteen she graduated from high school and went to nurses training in Galveston, but she didn't finish. Instead she got her emergency teaching certificate and taught at a school in Mission, Texas, for several years then became a Pan Am airline stewardess. But the love of family is what made her stop doing even that. So if I had to pinpoint her legacy, I would say it is her kids. I believe

Flo Rae Argersinger and daughter, Kitty, in Japan

Flo Rae Argersinger and daughter, Kitty, high school years

the biggest legacy you can pass on to the world is to have productive children, and I think it's remarkable she had six children who are all functioning in society. I've never heard her say she wished she had done something else. Never. No, she always wanted a big family and a bunch of kids, and basically she has given her whole life to that.

She laughs about how, when she first got married, she was obsessed with keeping the house clean until she realized it wasn't worth giving up time with her children just to scrub the floor or do an extra load of laundry. So she decided to stop anything she was doing if we needed her. Now she wasn't into playing games, but she always went outside with me if I wanted to ride my bike, and she does that with my two kids.

You know, I think the biggest gift she gives me is helping with our kids. When they are with her I don't think twice about whether they're being taken care of. I never think about them crying when I leave them, because I know they're happy. She always says that kids are a joy, and Mom doesn't make mountains out of molehills. To her everything is fixable, everything's do-able. I think if you choose to have as many kids as she did, then it is an automatic given she has patience and is caring. I remember when our daughter was little I'd say, "Oh, I can't wait until she can walk," or "I can't wait until she's not in diapers," something like that. And Mom would say, "Don't wish her life away."

Mom's a touchy-feely person and likes to hug. I remember her telling me that when I was little my hands felt like magic to her. When I was four or five years old, I used to love to rub my mom's legs because she had varicose veins, and I'd do something called "giving her the treatment." I'd rub her legs with lotion then take a tissue and lay it on top of her legs and pretend I was helping her varicose veins. I'd pat the tissue then peel it off and she'd say, "Oh, that feels so much better. Your hands feel like magic."

Speaking of hands, the favorite tangible gift she ever gave me is my engagement ring, which was hers. So that is a gift directly from her hands. But something more intangible is Mom's way of thinking it is better to laugh than to cry. She'd say that if you're frustrated with something, you need to laugh and find the humor in it, that is, of course, unless it is a funeral or something like that.

For example, when her mother, my Nannaw, was in a nursing home, that was hard on Mom because her mother had been so independent all her life. Mom got frustrated then but still she went to the nursing home every day. As Nannaw's health deteriorated, it was harder for Mom, but she was able to turn even that into a happy thing. Every Friday afternoon Mom would go to the nursing home and wheel the residents into the community room and have happy hour for them. She'd bring wine for those who could drink, and cheese and crackers for those who couldn't, and she'd take a tape recorder and play music. That was her way of laughing instead of crying.

Mom says she's lucky to have had so many kids and grandkids, and I've told her I feel so thankful for having someone like her to count on. You know, one of my favorite things about my mother is that she is so dependable. I can always count on her no matter what that if she says she's going to

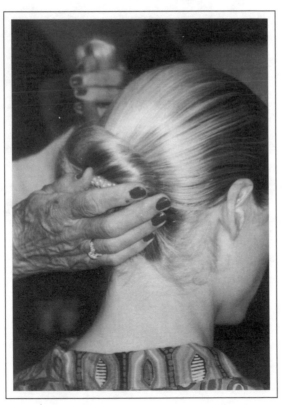

Flo Rae Argersinger fixing Kitty's hair for wedding, 1993

Kitty and Flo Rae Argersinger at Kitty's wedding to David Mellenbruch, 1993

167

be somewhere at a certain time, she'll be there. If she says she's going to do something, she'll do it. Whenever she makes a commitment, she'll keep it, and that's an admirable quality. You know, I don't think you truly appreciate your mother until you have children, because I don't think you realize what it takes to rear them. And to think of my mom having six kids, I just don't know how she did it physically, mentally, or emotionally.

I don't know what I'll do without her, but I try not to think on those lines. I mean when you call someone several times a day and when you see them every day, what happens when they're not there anymore? I tell her I can't do without her, but she says, "Oh, yes you can, it just might be more difficult, but you could do it." But I don't think I could.

Mom's soul is generous and without regret, and I think I'd describe her soul as the color yellow because it's so bright. In fact she loves sunsets more than sunrises because she finds them more colorful. Since I was little we have gone to the beach almost every summer and crabbed and fished and played. But one image I always see in my mind is of me playing in the background, picking up shells, and looking over and seeing Mom. There might be different people in and out of the scene, but there she is sitting at the water's edge in her yellow bathing suit with an ice chest full of boiled crabs beside her. And she is eating crabs, throwing their shells back in the ocean to feed the other animals, and seagulls are all around. And it is sunset.

Flo Rae Argersinger at beach, 1983

I hope I am like my mom. I hope that someday my kids can turn around and say I am the most dependable, loving person in their lives and that they know I'll always be there for them.

Pickled Okra

Pack okra in sterile pint jars tightly.

Bring to boil:
- 1 qt. white vinegar
- ½ c. salt
- 1 c. water
- 1 tsp. dill seed

Pack desired number of hot peppers plus 2 cloves of fresh garlic in each jar. Pour vinegar mixture over okra. Seal. Makes 4 quarts.

Shrimp Gumbo

- 1 lb. bacon
- 1 lb. okra
- 2 large onions
- Package of garlic
- 2 bay leaves
- 2 c. tomato sauce
- 2 lb. shrimp
- 1 tsp. chili powder

Cut bacon in small pieces; fry with onions until onions are clear. Add minced garlic and sauté. Add okra cut in small rounds. Add tomato sauce, small amount of water, chili powder, and bay leaves. Cook 15 minutes. Add shrimp and boil for 3 minutes. Turn off heat. Let sit, uncovered, for 30 minutes. Simmer. Makes 6 servings.

Rice Casserole

Melt 2 sticks oleo or butter. Sauté 2 medium onions in it. Combine with:
- 2 c. uncooked white rice
- 2 c. bouillon or consommé soup
- 1 c. water
- *(Add green pepper and pimientos for color.)*

Cook in covered casserole in a 350-degree oven for 1 hour.

Carrot Cake

8¾ oz. can crushed pineapple
3 c. all-purpose flour
2 c. sugar
1½ tsp. baking soda
1 tsp. baking powder
½ tsp. salt
2 tsp. ground cinnamon
3 large eggs
1½ c. corn oil
2 tsp. vanilla
2 c. coarsely shredded carrots
1½ c. broken pecans

Grease 10" x 4" tube pan. Drain pineapple (save syrup). Mix flour, sugar, baking soda, baking powder, salt, and cinnamon. Make well in center of bowl mixture and put in eggs, oil, pineapple syrup, and vanilla. Beat at medium speed till blended. With spoon stir in pecans, carrots, and pineapple. Turn into prepared pan. Bake in preheated 325 degree oven about 1½ hours. Cool 10 minutes. Then turn on rack to cool.

Kitty Argersinger Mellenbruch

A walk on the land at the Mellenbruch Ranch delights the senses. Close your eyes and listen to the whispers and songs of open spaces as they combine in concert. Breathe deeply and smell the aromatic black-bottom soil as it arouses images of abundance. With your bare hands, dig deeply into the rich loam and enjoy as it connects you to the world. Open wide your mouth to eat the air as the savory wind tingles your taste buds. Then let your eyes scan the expanse and follow this rolling landscape as it dips downward into lowlands then rides upward to the hillcrests. This is a natural paradise that offers earthen gifts, and its matriarch, Kitty Argersinger Mellenbruch, is a woman who lends her soul to the place.

Physically imposing as she stands taller than most women, Kitty is a natural beauty, a salt-of-the-earth woman whose feet are solidly planted. Her practical wisdom underlies the directness with which she cares for her husband, family, ranch, and careers. Combine her inherited mother wit with strong ethics and you have a woman who's both hale and honorable. Kitty approaches work—whether on the home front or in the classroom —

believing that only out of sweat and toil can one be proud of the fruits of one's labors.

Kitty was born in Misawa, Japan, at the air force base where her father was stationed and spent the first years of her life on foreign soil. Then in keeping with many military families the Argersingers moved to air force bases in Virginia and Texas with their last home being in Del Valle, Texas.

It was during her later years at Del Valle High School that Kitty met and fell in love with David Mellenbruch, whom she married in 1993. Since 1991 Kitty has taught high school English in the Eanes Independent School District, but in the midst of things she and David became parents of a daughter, Meagan, and a son, Justin.

Kitty, along with her husband, David, is also a juggler of business endeavors. One business, although now defunct, was in the goat industry. Influenced by David's grandfather, who raised Tennessee wooden legs, Kitty found she enjoyed helping and upon his death was left with his herd. The Mellenbruchs then purchased thirty-five Nubians and a buck, bringing Lecheras (milkmaids) Farms to

Kitty Mellenbruch and daughter, Meagan, Christmas 1999

life. They then began selling to breeders, dairies, and individuals until their daughter was born and Kitty auctioned off the goats in order to have more time for motherhood.

Today the Mellenbruchs have approximately eighty cows and run a cow-calf operation, performing all worming, dehorning, castrating, vaccinating, and branding themselves. Maximizing the land yearly, Kitty and David plant ninety acres in coastal bermuda to produce about twenty thousand square bales of hay. Together they recently started ColorQuest to raise roughly eight thousand trees—live oaks, bur oaks, and crepe myrtles—for wholesale and have opened a retail business to sell the trees along with imported pottery.

In all, Kitty Argersinger Mellenbruch carries many calling cards—rancher, homemaker, educator, and businesswoman. But at Kitty's core lies her true identity inherited from her mother, Flo Rae, and that is "Earth Mother" in the broadest sense.

Lois Palfrey and daughter, Evelyn Palfrey

Lois Evelyn Palfrey

b. 1926

It's just amazing about becoming our mothers, but I'm not dismayed over that. If I would actually become my mother, that would be a good thing. In fact, I've said to her that she is the woman I would like to be.

MOTHER HAS A STRONG SENSE OF DUTY, which was shaped in large measure from being a minister's child. She talks about how their home was open to church members because the parsonage belonged to the church. So I think her sense of duty was shaped by that. I guess because Mother was thrust into the role of the older child, she is attuned to duty. Now she doesn't want to be the president and does not have a lot to do with meetings and discussions, but if there's something that needs to be done, then Mother's going to do it.

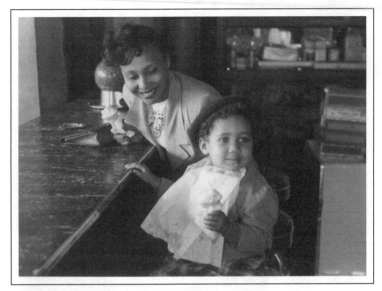

Lois and Evelyn Palfrey

There was only one high school on the edge of the small segregated town where I grew up, and Mother was the home economics teacher there. A lot of the social life revolved around the school, and it usually fell to the Home Ec department to provide refreshments for functions. Anything that needed done Mother did. It was the same at church where she provided the Christmas tree cookies. I mean we always had these cookies, and we laugh about how, even though they might be in different shapes for other occasions, we always called them the Christmas tree cookies. Another image of Mother and her sense of duty is related to the time my grandmother took ill and Mother felt she needed to make sure her mother wasn't alone. So her mother was moved in to live with us, and I don't remember Mother complaining in any way about that.

That just goes hand in hand with the one word I think describes Mother—persistence. When she decides something is going to be, you may as well give in and do it right off the top because she has a staying power that is beyond human. I'm serious. You might as well give in to her. It's just her approach to life, but she isn't just insisting on her own way, she's insisting because she has your best interest at heart. I'd say she is like a fox because she's so cunning and will get her way and will be gracious about it.

Evelyn Palfrey and mother, Lois Palfrey

Now Mother is only about five feet tall, but here is this little woman who's bigger than life.

Throughout everything Mother is the peacekeeper. Sometimes you feel you just need to air things out, but Mother wants peace in the family, and she'll do whatever that takes. If you insist on bringing up old stuff and she thinks you're going to disturb the order, she's not going to let you do that. She's going to smooth things over, and I think that's admirable.

Now that I think about it, I guess Mother is also a protector. I didn't see that when I was a child because in those times there were just a

Lois Palfrey

lot of things children weren't privy to. I remember this one time I got crosswise with one of the adults at school, but Mother's line to me about the whole thing was, "That person's an adult and you're a child." Basically she was saying I needed to sit down and be quiet. It was only years later that I found out my mother had actually put her own job in jeopardy to defend me, but I didn't see that, I heard about that. And since there was only one school, where else would she have worked? So when I heard how Mother had taken up for me at school, I saw her as a lioness protecting me at the chance of costing her a job. It's interesting. My parents didn't tell us a lot that they loved us, but they showed us. Mother's whole life was wrapped up in us, and I don't think she expected to have a life of her own because she saw it as her duty to be a mother.

I remember when the library in Texarkana was initially integrated, which meant that black children could come in and check out books but couldn't stay and read. Now my parents saw it as their solemn duty to make sure we got books out of that library every Saturday, and I think I probably read every book in it. Mother made sure of that, and I feel like I owe part of my love of reading and writing to Mother.

I write under Mother's name and feel it's important she approves my work because I want her to be comfortable since I create romances for mature women. Now growing up you have to understand my sex education had been pretty limited. Back then we didn't have folks making babies on television. I think all I knew about sex was that I wasn't to "let the little boys take me under the house," so you see I really didn't understand about sex. Well, at age forty-five when I was writing the first book, I sent her a couple of chapters after I got them where I kind of wanted them. She read those chapters and asked me to send her the next one. So I sent it, but because it had some pretty explicit sex in it I wasn't sure what she'd say.

Now you have to remember that by the time I wrote this book I had been married twice and had two kids, but there was still this wall up about sex. Anyway I sent her the chapter and gritted my teeth. After a while I called to ask what she thought, and she said, "Oh, it was good. Send me the next chapter." Then I asked her what she REALLY thought, and she said, "I *said* it was good." I said, "Mother, what did you think about the SEX?" She just died laughing and said, "Girl, what sex? What have you been reading? What you wrote was nothing." So Mother surprises me.

About ten years ago, a short time after my father died, I realized we can have a sudden loss and not have all this time we think we have to say all the words we want to say. So I sat down and wrote Mother a letter. I thanked her for how she did my hair when I was growing up—washing it, plaiting it, and pressing it, which was a very time-consuming process for black women. Then when I got old enough to do it myself, I cut it all off and she didn't voice one word of complaint. I thanked her for the wedding dress she made me and how it is one of my favorite gifts from her. And for the gift of reading, the sense of duty, and for a lot of things. And I told her how much I admire her.

Mother has a definite view about what the world is, where she fits in, and where everybody else fits in. She's certain about that, and I think as long as it all works out, then her soul is at peace, at rest, and nothing needs fixing.

My mother taught home economics and was responsible for providing refreshments for many school functions. She was also active with the church and several social and community service organizations, so it seemed Mama always had copious quantities of her seasonal cookies on hand for any occasion. I'll bet my sister and I ate thousands of Mama's cookies, not to mention a mountain of cookie dough.

Lois Palfrey's Seasonal Cookies

> 1 c. butter
> ¾ c. sugar
> 1 egg
> 2¼ c. flour
> ⅛ tsp. salt
> ¼ tsp. baking powder
> 1 tsp. almond or vanilla extract
> Food coloring

Cream butter, adding sugar gradually. Add unbeaten egg. Sift dry ingredients. Add dry ingredients, flavoring, and a few drops of food coloring. Mix well. Press through a cookie shaper onto an ungreased cookie sheet. Bake at 375 degrees for 10 to 12 minutes.

One night my daddy commented the weekly tuna casserole tasted a little different. We all agreed but continued eating. None of us could quite put our finger on what was different until finally Daddy said, "Lois, I don't believe there's any tuna in this tuna casserole." Sure enough, two open cans of tuna were on the counter by the stove. For nearly forty years, we have not let the home economics teacher forget the tuna-less casserole.

Lois Palfrey's Quick Tuna Casserole

> 2 c. macaroni
> Chopped onion, bell pepper, celery
> 1 can your choice of cream soup (mushroom, celery, etc.)
> ½ c. milk
> 2 cans tuna
> Salt, pepper

Cook macaroni in water until nearly done. Sauté onion, bell pepper, and celery in skillet in butter. Drain macaroni, pour into casserole dish. Add onion, bell pepper, and celery. Mix in cream soup, milk, than tuna. Season to taste. Bake uncovered in 350-degree oven until hot and bubbly.

Evelyn Palfrey

They say that if you work hard to find a balance in your life between work and play, you'll be all the healthier for it. If that bears credence, then Evelyn Palfrey must be feeling mighty healthy these days. Her world is one that many adults often envy as she has found that ground between two worlds—the world of law and the world of romance writing.

Evelyn Palfrey, 1996

Knowing that Evelyn combines these two worlds successfully, I was curious to figure out what made her tick. As I drove up to her family's house, I first noticed the fastidiously manicured lawn, and upon entering the home I saw an interior just as meticulously kept. Then I heard one giant squawk, yet Evelyn didn't miss a stride in what she was saying. Then came another squawk and again Evelyn talked on. I cut my eyes to look for the culprit, but not until we stepped into the family room did I spy the source. Back in the far corner of the dining room, a brilliant green Quaker parrot squawked upon her perch, and over the course of two hours as Evelyn shared her mother stories, we were accompanied by the sporadic gibbering of Mahti, the parrot.

Evelyn Palfrey grew up in Texarkana, graduated from Southern Methodist University in Dallas, and later received a Doctorate of Jurisprudence from the University of Texas Law School in Austin. Utilizing her background in law, Evelyn has served on the Travis County Lawyer Referral Service, the State Bar of Texas, the board of directors of the Texas Municipal Court Education Center, and the Legal Aspects of the Arts Committee of the State Bar of Texas.

But that is only one side of Evelyn, who by day works in the criminal justice system and by night writes mature romance novels. She explains that to her "romance is just as beautiful with a little gray at the temples and a little fullness in places that used to be flat" and that there is a "challenge and joy at every stage of life." Incorporated into her romantic tales are mature heroines and heroes whose ordeals result in happy endings.

She has written three romance novels: *Three Perfect Men*, *The Price of Passion*, and *Dangerous Dilemmas*, all of which were self-published through her company, Moon Child Books. *The Price of Passion* and *Dangerous Dilemmas* were listed on the Blackboard bestseller list in *Essence* magazine. Evelyn has signed a multibook contract with Pocket Books, a division of Simon & Schuster.

Evelyn has served on the board of directors of the Austin Writers' League, is a member of that same league, and is active with the Austin Romance Writers of America.

It was interesting to meet this woman whose daily life offers the best of two worlds—one of measure, rationality, and level-headedness, and the other of desire, emotion, and flights of fancy. And so to know Evelyn Palfrey is to know balance.

Dee Parker-Davies and daughter, Janie Parker

Dee Parker-Davies

b. 1923

I don't have just one single special moment with my mother, but something of hers I love is this gorgeous fairy tale book she had from her childhood. You know it's funny that I grew up to dance ballets, which are basically fairy tales, so it was like her book just opened up and came to life on stage and I got to dance inside her book.

GEORGE BALANCHINE ONCE SAID that in order to create a dancer, a child should have good childhood literature and music in the home, and both should start by the age of eight. Well in our home my parents—who were both great intellects and music lovers—definitely had great childhood literature and musicians around the house.

They were avid readers, and I'm sure that's why I loved to read. And I remember my father loved opera and my mother was a very good pianist.

You know, I can still see Mama's hands on the piano keys. Anyway I was around literature and music and I started ballet all by the time I was eight years old, so I guess you could say my mother and father shaped the world that led to my becoming a ballerina.

Mama was the one who suggested I go to the North Carolina School of the Arts, which meant going away from home at the age of thirteen, but she would do anything to facilitate it because I wanted it so much. She would have loved it if I had turned into a pianist or a teacher like her, but I wanted to dance. I was drawn to it, and once I started there was no stopping. So she was happy to support that and never made me feel bad about what I wanted to do.

Mother is always supportive. She is one hundred percent in my court in every area of my life. I think of her as a mama bear, a mama lion, and she is going to protect her baby and do it one hundred percent. You might call that a figurative gift, but I think the greatest gift she has given me is her complete, unconditional love and support.

Because she is so supportive in everything, it came right through in my ballet. During hours of practice, she would just hang out and maybe grade school papers, but she'd just be there. I always felt like there was someone nearby who was proud of me, and that felt nice. She'd be there at the theater waiting for me and always ready to go to anything no matter how tired she might be. You know I knew a lot of people whose parents were not there for things in their lives, so this was very important to me.

When I was younger I don't think I was aware that it was such a treasured gift to have a parent as supportive as she was. I think I took it for granted. But about halfway through my career it occurred to me that I was lucky to have somebody who believed in me so strongly. I know that if I were to have children, I would replicate as closely as I could my mother's attitude towards me because I feel it was that positive in my life.

In a sense, I think I've gotten my love for physical affection from Mama. It obviously was important that she hugged me a lot because to this day I am a huggy and affectionate woman. And her tenderness is such that if you have a headache or a sore muscle, she rubs your head or back. In fact, during my whole childhood when she woke me and my sister, she would gently rub little circles with her hands on our backs and say softly, "I'm stirring your blood."

I think it would be accurate to say the seed of everything my mother has given me stems from love. Mama has always said I love you, and that's the best thing you can hear from somebody. I can hear her now, "I love you, Sweetie Heart." Because I have felt loved I am able to broaden my scope, and I tend to want to love as openly as I perceive she did. To me this whole world is just a big candy store filled with so many people, and I get to love everybody. As I grew up I realized that everything is about love, and that is a great gift my mother allowed me.

Mother is a good listener, and I believe I would also call her a mediator. She truly dislikes discord and admits she has a Pollyanna attitude and just never invests in the darker side.

Dee Parker-Davies

She sees and wants life to be positive, and I think I adopted that attitude from her. She is always going to try to sort things out and find the solution in a positive way. I guess you could say she doesn't so much do the devil's advocate, but she does the angel's advocate.

In keeping with her angel-like quality, I'd say another term that describes Mama's nature is she's a giver. She's just so giving and helpful to others and sees absolutely no value in putting some people on the outside of the fence. She has this attitude that when you get right down to it we are all the brotherhood of mankind. My mama, actually both parents, exhibited a lack of prejudice to the nth degree. With my father it was the Quaker background, and with my mother it was that she taught in a school that was seventy-five percent black back in the days when there were segregated schools. They never really spoke about prejudice, I just know about the lack of prejudice because of watching and learning from their actions and behaviors. That was just the value system I grew up with and came to believe in and appreciate.

Whenever I'm depressed I find myself wanting my mama, and if I can't be with her since she lives so far away, I often get down one of my scrapbooks she made and look through it. She made my first scrapbook after my first recital and gave it to me on my ninth birthday. That birthday present kind of kept going until she has done scrapbooks covering my entire career, so that's thirty-two years of dancing she has documented in around twenty-five scrapbooks. I guess that's her legacy she's leaving me, all the scrapbooks and memoirs and memories.

I could tell Mama anything in my life and she was there for me. Sometimes we didn't agree, but I had no fear of telling her. I feel fortunate that I have a friend in my mother. I see Mama as an independent, fearless woman, and if I were to dance her spirit or soul it would be bubbly allegro with moments of tender adagio.

Mama made up this recipe box for me my last year in New York when I got my own place. She wanted me to have recipes from things I grew up with, you know, when you're out on your own and missing home. So they're comfort foods because they're Mama's.

Chicken and Vegetable Casserole

I can cream of chicken soup
I can water
½ c. regular rice or ¾ c. minute rice
¼ tsp. salt
Small can cooked, boned chicken.

Mix above ingredients together; put ½ in bottom of casserole dish. Cover this layer with ½ cup diced celery, I small chopped onion, and about 3 carrots cut into strips. Add rest of chicken-rice mixture. Cover with bay leaves and bake covered for 1¼ hours in 350-degree oven. During last 15 minutes, put sliced green pepper rings on top. Serves 6.

Potato Salad

3 to 4 potatoes, boiled and diced
3 hard-boiled eggs, diced
3 stalks celery, sliced
8-10 radishes, sliced
5-6 small green onions

Boil potatoes for 15-20 minutes. Boil eggs about 15 minutes. Mix all ingredients together with about 3 Tbsp. of mayonnaise. Calories: 960 total; 240 per serving. Total grams protein: 28 total, 7 per serving. Servings: 4.

Thousand Island Dressing

Mix together:

    3 hard-boiled eggs, chopped
    I c. chili sauce
    I Tbsp. chopped parsley
    I Tbsp. chopped olives
    I Tbsp. chopped sweet pickle
    I small can pimiento, chopped
    I green pepper, chopped

Add 2 cups of mayonnaise and $\frac{1}{3}$ cup salad oil. Mix well.

Janie Parker

Janie Parker as the Merry Widow (Houston Ballet)
Photograph by Jim Caldwell

There are people in this world who gladden your heart just by their presence, and Janie Parker is such a person. The minute you meet her, your soul somersaults and suddenly you feel like dancing. Perhaps it is her innocence? Perhaps it is her whimsicality? Regardless, Janie captivates you with her joyful nature.

I should know because on the night of the interview, my brother Gary and I headed through the myriad Houston streets to find her neighborhood. In the evening's darkness we had difficulty deciphering the system for the house numbers that seemingly held no rhyme or reason, a task made even more taxing due to the absence of streetlights.

Once the house was located I waved good-bye to Gary, and the minute I stepped into Janie's home all frustrations were vanquished by her enthusiasm. As we sat for two hours in her garage studio, Janie Parker,

185

ever the dancer, choreographed her range of feelings for her mother. One moment she would be enlivened by a funny event they had shared and the next a tenderness would overtake her, brought on by a remembrance. Yet in all she shared about her life as a ballerina, the one common thread woven throughout was that of her mother as champion.

Janie Parker started her career in 1973 dancing with Le Grand Ballet du Gran Theatre de Geneve, a Balanchine satellite company. During her second year with the company she was promoted to soloist and danced many leading ballet roles such as *Concerto Barroco*, *Apollo*, and *Agon*. During her third year with the company, Ben Stevenson brought his production of *Cinderella* to the repertoire and chose Janie for the title role. When Mr. Stevenson became the artistic director of the Houston Ballet, Janie joined him as a soloist in the company and in her third year was promoted to principal dancer.

During the twenty years she danced for Ben Stevenson, he created many roles for her—Juliet from *Romeo and Juliet*, Mimi from *Miraculous Mandarin*, and Alice from *Alice in Wonderland*. Janie also danced the leading role in classics such as *Swan Lake*, *Sleeping Beauty*, and *The Nutcracker*. She has also danced before Princess Margaret, Princess Grace, King Olav, Fidel Castro, and audiences from all over the United States, Mexico, Canada, Europe, Scandinavia, Russia, Japan, China, and Chile.

In 1981 Janie Parker was the first American female to win a gold medal in the Senior Women's Division of the International Ballet Competition. Then after twenty-three years, Janie danced her final professional performance on June 15, 1996, as Aurora in Houston Ballet's production of *Sleeping Beauty*.

Currently, Janie performs in stage plays, works as a Pilates instructor, and often teaches Mr. Stevenson's ballets to other companies. She occasionally lectures on the subject of her career and her transition into other roles. And a special project of Janie's is working with her mother on a book, a book that can be written because her mother, Dee Parker-Davis, began documenting Janie's dancing career that began when she was but a child. And so for over thirty years, Ms. Davies has collected, cut, and pasted mementos into scrapbook after scrapbook after scrapbook—as a gift from a mother's hands to those of her daughter, Janie Parker.

Dadie Stillwell Potter

rancher; educator

Dadie Potter and mother, Hallie, on Stillwell Ranch, 1987

Hallie Marie Crawford Stillwell

b. 1897

If I could thank Mama for only three things, I would thank her for the land and the family and the optimism she has passed on to me.

MAMA'S MOTHER WAS A SOUTHERN WOMAN and particular about wanting Mama to be a lady, but she was a tomboy who just adored her father and followed him around all the time. The housework and cooking and sewing weren't for her, no, those were for her older sister Mable. When Mama graduated from high school with her primary certificate, she wanted to go to Presidio to teach because they paid ten dollars more a month for hazard pay and so that meant she'd make about seventy dollars a month. She approached her father for twenty-five dollars to get started, and he said he thought she was going on a wild goose chase. But Mama knew

Hallie Marie Crawford Stillwell

Hallie Stillwell, Presidio, Texas, 1916

what she wanted to do, and she had a vision so she said, "Well then, I'll gather my geese."

Later she met my father, they married and moved onto his ranch, and Mama began a whole new life. There were three of us kids, me and my brothers Son and Guy, and since Mama was so family oriented, she wanted everybody to know each other and always tried to keep us close. She was happiest when we had family reunions because we'd sit around and talk about everything, and the more she could gather people in, the happier she was. She just had many friends who admired her; Mama liked to have a good time with them all, and laughter was just a part of that.

Mama was resourceful. She always came up with something to earn extra money so she could provide us with better things. When we were little the school put in a cafeteria, and most kids got free lunches, but we owned land so we didn't get them. Well Mama put in a beauty shop in order to be able to pay for our school lunches. She was, I would say, strong, and she accomplished many things because of her strong will. She didn't care how hard she had to work. I can still see her in the branding pen helping my father and the boys, working right alongside them tailing the calves and tying their feet together. And I remember once when she built a bathroom all by herself. Every once in a while I'd help her, you know, hand her a board or something, but she was the one who built it.

But she was also feminine. She always wore a hat and a scarf around her neck. She wore makeup and kept her fingernails polished and always wore gloves to protect her hands from the sun when she rode horseback. I remember when we'd go someplace in the car, she'd even cover her hands from the sun with her skirt so she wouldn't get those brown spots. She just stayed feminine even though she worked like a man.

Mama has such pretty hands, and when I think of them I also see her writing. She wrote a newspaper column called "Ranch News" for the *Alpine Avalanche* for years and years. And I used to watch her write her notes. Then for her book *I'll Gather My Geese*, I can still see her writing it in longhand on her yellow tablets. She autographed thousands of those books. Every time someone would come into the store and buy one, she'd sit down and write something in it. So I can just see her with a pencil in her hand, writing the news or autographing books.

Hallie Stillwell and ranch cowboy

I think Mother was the original Scarlett O'Hara. She would sleep on things. When she'd have a problem, she'd go to bed and believe that tomorrow would be better. So I guess one of my strongest images is of her common sense and positive outlook on life, which was "Just hang on. It'll change. Some day it'll rain." I know that when my kids or I have a crisis, we try to think what my mama, what Hallie would do. Because of her, we're pretty optimistic.

And Mama was a visionary. She foresaw how things would work and she gambled with life. After my father died, she had a vision of turning the ranch into an RV park and a store. She went to the banker, but he wouldn't lend her the money. Then she told a nephew about her idea—but didn't ask for money—and not too long after he returned to California, he sent Mama five thousand dollars with no strings attached.

She got busy and before long the park and store were built. You see, she had vision.

Mama believed everybody should get an education, I don't remember her ever helping with homework, but she would take me out and we'd go down into the canyons where the Indians had been and hunt for arrowheads. It would be so quiet, but I can hear her talking about the canyon, the Indians, the paintings, and the ceremonial caves and I just learned a lot from her.

Hallie's 94th birthday, October 20, 1991—at dedication of Hallie's Hall of Fame Museum

Mama did a lot of talking to groups and colleges about ranch life and ropes and branding irons, and she'd tell her true stories. She had a wonderful memory and never forgot a thing. I miss her being here, greeting people and telling those stories. When I'm in the museum talking about her and her stories, I feel like she's with me, like I can hear her soft voice.

Mama was in a nursing home the last ten months of her life, and I had planned a big party for her one hundredth birthday. I had made arrangements for the home to bring her to the party, but she died on a morning in August, two months before her birthday.

Mama had lived her life and was just tired, so we knew her death was coming. But it was still hard to take. Since she always had family or friends around, we went ahead and had a big celebration, but it was the strangest thing. Six white geese flew over right before the program started, and everybody just thought Hallie wanted to let us know she was there with us.

I can still feel Mama, see her, especially walking down the road with her walking stick. Mama had an old soul. She was here for so long and saw so many changes—electricity, telephones, and airplanes—and she was tickled she got to see all those things. She always said she lived in the best era of life and she wouldn't have wanted to live in any other time.

Mama loved the mountains because they were her security. She'd say when she woke up and looked out she knew they'd always be there. They were a constant in life and always put you in your place in the grand scheme of things. To her we are just their caretakers.

1, 2, 3, 4 Cake

Ahead of time: Preheat oven to 325 degrees. Lightly grease and flour three cake pans (9-inch round).

1 c. butter
2 c. sugar
3 c. flour
4 eggs
1 tsp. salt
3 tsp. baking powder
1 c. milk
½ tsp. vanilla extract

Cream butter and sugar until light and fluffy. Add eggs one at a time, beating well after each. Sift flour, salt, and baking powder two or three times. Add flour mixture and milk alternately to creamed mixture, beating well each time. Mix in the vanilla.

Pour batter into prepared pans and bake 25 to 30 minutes at 350 degrees. Layers will begin to pull away from sides of pan when done.

Cool layers 5 to 10 minutes in pans, then remove to wire racks to finish cooling (keep bottom sides of layers next to the rack).

Makes a nice-sized cake. Ice with your favorite frosting. You can also add almond extract in addition to the vanilla.

Sugar Cookies

    1 c. butter
    1 ½ c. powdered sugar
    1 egg
    1 tsp. vanilla
    ½ tsp. almond flavoring

Combine:
    1 tsp. baking powder
    1 tsp. cream of tartar
    3 c. flour

Mix ingredients in order. Mixture will be crumbly. Knead with your hands on table. If it is too dry, add 1 or 2 tablespoons of milk. No need to refrigerate. Roll out and cut with cookie cutter. Bake 7 to 8 minutes in oven at 375 degrees. Ice and enjoy.

Frozen Fruit - Nut Salad

    ½ c. pecans
    2 c. sour cream
    ½ c. sugar
    8 oz. crushed, drained pineapple
    1 diced banana
    ½ tsp. salt
    2 Tbsp. lemon juice

Mix ingredients and put in freezer.

Fruitcake Balls

    1 can Eagle Brand milk
    1 lb. dates, chopped
    4 oz. candied cherries, chopped
    4 c. pecans, coarsely chopped
    1 c. coconut
    2 tsp. vanilla

Put all ingredients in large bowl. Mix together by hand. Roll into balls the size of a walnut. Bake on a greased cookie sheet for 25 minutes at 300 degrees.

Chalupa Loaf

1-1½ lb. ground beef
1 tsp. salt
2 Tbsp. chili powder
⅓ c. chopped green bell pepper
⅓ c. chopped onion
1 c. evaporated milk
1 c. tomato sauce
10 corn tortillas
½ lb. grated cheese

Brown meat and add salt, chili powder, green pepper, and onions. Simmer until onion is tender. Drain fat. Add milk and tomato sauce. Cut tortillas into strips and alternate layers of tortillas, meat, and cheese. Reserve some cheese for the top. Bake at 300 degrees for approximately 40 minutes.

Dadie Stillwell Potter

Dadie Stillwell Potter
Photo courtesy of James H. Evans, Evans Gallery, Marathon, Texas

A coolness blanketed the early morning air as I stepped from the camper's trailer reserved for guests at the Stillwell Ranch located at the edge of Big Bend National Park. Charmed by the trailer's porch swing, I took a seat and with one foot pushed against the ground to start a gentle rocking, then I stared. Stared out at the outstretched land rolling in brown and gray and green waves that peaked as distant hills and canyon cliffs surged up to salute this beautiful Texas territory. The spaciousness unfolded and I daydreamed of exploring this desert where thousands of years before American Indians had lived. In mid-reverie, a quiet conversation drifted over, and I rose to say good morning to my hostess, Dadie Stillwell Potter.

Behind the store Ignacio, the ranch hand, and Dadie drank coffee. He tipped his straw hat in greeting, she gave a short wave with her hand, and both offered me a cup of coffee. I accepted then pulled up a chair, and the three of us talked while kittens romped about. Not a bad way to start the day, I commented, and they nodded. Then Ignacio announced it was time for breakfast, and soon we were joined at the table by Dadie's daughter, Linda Perron, a family friend, John Miller, and a writer who had also made the trip, Karen Casey Fitzjerrell.

Life is good for Dadie Stillwell Potter, who was born in nearby Marathon, Texas, in 1921. She spent most of her childhood with her two brothers —Son and Guy—and mother and father on the ranch where life consisted of upkeep and working cattle. Her mother, Hallie, wanted the children to receive a good education, so a house was bought in Marathon and they lived there during the week, returning to the ranch on weekends, holidays, and summers.

After high school Dadie attended Our Lady of the Lake College in San Antonio, Texas, and received a bachelor's degree in physical education, health, and science. She began teaching but left two years later when she married W. T. Potter and started a family. After five children and nine years, she returned to the classroom and secured a master's degree from Sul Ross University. Dadie taught for thirty-two years—twenty-eight of those in the Northeast Independent School District in San Antonio. During that time she initiated and coached golf at Garner Middle School and helped start a driver's education program.

After retiring in 1983 Dadie returned to the ranch and her beloved Brewster County. Presently she and her husband own the Stillwell Store, an RV park, and eleven sections of land. They still run cattle, but her biggest pride is the Hallie's Hall of Fame Museum, which keeps her mother's memory alive. Daughter Linda and Dadie take on the role as museum docent with anyone who visits and wants to learn about Hallie Stillwell's life. And today there are plans for Dadie's four living children to move to the ranch when they retire. Alongside their mother, Dadie Stillwell Potter, they will help keep the Stillwell family legacy alive.

Louise Raggio

attorney

Hilma Matilda Lindgren Ballerstedt

b. 1885

I knew Mama really cared. There was never any question but that I was number one, and I knew she would have given the last drop of blood she had for me.

ALL OF MY GRANDPARENTS immigrated to the United States in the late 1800s and settled on adjoining farms east of Austin in Manor, Texas. Then my parents were born within three months of each other. Now in those days the immigrant kids couldn't start school until after the cotton had been picked and then they had to leave school when it was time to work the fields. This gave them only about four or five months of school. So Mother had about a sixth-grade education, which she received in a one-room building.

That was before radio and television, so these little communities had plays and programs regularly. By the time I was three years old Mother would clip poems to have me memorize. I remember standing on

Hilma Matilda Lindgren Ballerstedt

a chair and going over something until it was perfect then doing it for company. And she taught me to project. She would stand in the back and say, "Now you get your voice out to the back row." I think I was the only kid that did these declarations every time there was a program in this whole area. You see, what Mama wanted, Mama got.

Now Mama was not an actress, but I was doing what she wished she could have done. She channeled her energy into me, and I performed whether I wanted to or not. And I remember I never went to school that I hadn't gone over all my spelling and reading. We'd work in the kitchen because she was always doing something in there, and she'd make sure I knew it perfectly. I went to a two-room school for the first seven grades then to Manor for a few years. When I got to Austin High School it was during the depths of the Depression.

During those hard times, my uncle had a one-bedroom home with a parlor, so my mother, Daddy, and I moved into the parlor. My uncle was a wonderful cabinetmaker, but there wasn't much work for cabinet people. Daddy was lucky and got a laborer's job on the county road that paid him either seventy-five or ninety dollars a month, and that was the only income for the two families. Even though I came out of the country very underprivileged, I was valedictorian of Austin High School and later graduated number two in my class at the University of Texas in Austin.

I guess you could say Mother just basked in all my honors, and I know all I did were vicarious achievements for her. You see, I was the first farm kid in our whole area who went to college. Anyway Mother took a lot of flack about wasting money on a higher education, especially on a girl, but I worked my way through college with Mother there taking care of my clothes and backing me up. I don't know if it was fear or what, but I durn sure knew I'd better aspire and achieve. Mother and Daddy gave me everything they were capable of, and I know they went without so I could have things. You see, some years we didn't make five hundred dollars on the farm, but Mama made sure to give me an education.

My mother's grandfather was a tailor from Sweden. In those days there weren't any ready-to-wear shops in this community, so the tailors would stay with a farm family for a week and make all the clothes. Mother was his apprentice, and she'd go with him and they'd work sewing up all the clothes. Mother could look at a dress in a store window then cut her own pattern and make a beautiful outfit. She became such a fabulous tailor and was the best seamstress I've ever known.

Mother was also the family nurse. But you see that was not unusual because if anybody got sick in the family, you had to take care of them. Her mother had asthma, and I can remember as far back as memory goes that Mother would go to nurse her. I knew I had to be quiet and good so I'd sit in the corner with some crayons. Much later in my life when I was in Washington, D.C., two friends came down with the flu during an epidemic, and I had to take care of them. I knew how to nurse them because I'd watched my mother, and it never occurred to me that it was anything different because I'd seen it all my life, just like I'd seen cooking all my life.

You have to give the old gal credit. She was intelligent and didn't have any questions about what she thought. You see, before I was born in 1919, she was the first woman in that community who learned to drive the old Model T Ford. She thought it was stupid that women couldn't drive and that it was ridiculous women couldn't vote. Now she was not a leader like some of the old suffragists, but she and her sister went all over the country talking to the farm men to get them to vote for suffrage. She was such a hell on wheels that I think Mother could have managed General Motors or run the Normandy invasion.

> *. . . she and her sister went all over the country talking to the farm men to get them to vote for suffrage. She was such a hell on wheels that I think Mother could have managed General Motors or run the Normandy invasion.*

I've been a lawyer since 1952 and listed in the Best Lawyers in America for years, but as far as Mama was concerned, that was just one step ahead of being a felon. She did not think it fitting for a woman to be a lawyer, period, and she told me so many times. She didn't mince words. She thought I should have stayed home and taken care of the kids. You see, I was supposed to be a schoolteacher, so when I became a lawyer she never softened, not to me. While she would brag to other people, she'd be damned if she'd ever tell me.

You know, I never was Mother's peer, and she was my boss even to the last. Mother left the farm when she was past ninety years old to stay with me in Dallas, but she didn't like it so she moved to a retirement home in Round Rock for the last eight or nine years of her life. Now she was at this retirement home and they had maybe three wheelchairs, and since I was always making gifts to the home, the director told me Mother really could use her own. So I stupidly went out and got the best one with bells and whistles. I can remember her taking one look at that wheelchair and right then—she was ninety-eight years old—I think she said to herself she wasn't going to be an invalid and sort of willed herself to die. I wasn't there when she died on Christmas Eve, but I was so glad that she could go peacefully, that she was spared an uncomfortable death.

Mother's legacy is me. I am what I am because of her. Obviously I had to have some engine to keep me going, and even though I was not going in the direction she wanted me to go, I always knew how important I was to her. If anything I was smothered in attention, but that's sure better than being neglected.

Cabbage Rolls

I large head cabbage
1 ¼ lb. round steak, ground very fine
I can tomato sauce
I large onion, minced
I clove garlic
2 or 3 sour salt crystals (citric acid or tartaric acid)
2 Tbsp. or more brown sugar
Stock or bouillon cubes

Put whole cabbage in pot of boiling water. Simmer five minutes. Remove and cool. Brown onion and garlic in butter. Put tomato sauce and 2 or 3 crystals of sour salt in. Add brown sugar. Add stock or bouillon cubes.

Peel leaves off cabbage. Mix onions and garlic with meat. Place I or 2 Tbsp. in leaves and roll up envelope fashion. Brown envelope in peanut oil. Place in casserole and pour tomato mixture over. Cover and bake 1 ½ hours at 275 degrees. Serve over rice. Cabbage should be transparent, silky brown.

Raisin Pie

2 c. raisins
2 c. water

½ c. brown sugar
2 Tbsp. cornstarch
1 tsp. cinnamon
⅛ tsp. salt
1 Tbsp. vinegar
1 Tbsp. butter

Boil raisins in 1½ cups of water. When done add remaining ingredients. Boil slowly. When thick, pour into baked piecrust. Bake 30 minutes at 350 degrees.

Waffles

Beat 2 egg whites until stiff. In another bowl, beat 2 egg yolks and then add 1 cup milk. Add scant 1½ cups sifted flour, 2 teaspoons baking powder, ½ teaspoon salt, and 2 teaspoons sugar. Then add ⅓ cup cooled melted butter. Fold in stiff egg whites. Cook in preheated waffle iron.

Ice Box Cookies

1 c. brown sugar
1 c. white sugar
1½ c. melted shortening
4½ c. flour
3 eggs (beaten)
2 tsp. baking soda
1 tsp. salt
1 tsp. cinnamon
1 c. pecans

Mix all ingredients and form into rolls. Put in icebox overnight. Slice thin. Bake in a 450 degree oven for 4 to 7 minutes (or until golden brown).

Peanut Butter Cookies

½ c. butter
½ c. white sugar
½ c. brown sugar
¾ tsp. baking powder
¼ tsp. baking soda
1½ c. flour
1 egg
½ c. peanut butter

Pinch of salt

Cream butter and peanut butter. Add egg and other ingredients. Cook in a hot oven.

Louise Raggio

Traffic on U.S. 75 in downtown Dallas snarled as construction funneled four lanes of cars into one stream, so it was a relief when I turned onto Lemmon Avenue where things became calmer. Within blocks I spied the law office of Raggio and Raggio, but before heading inside I reviewed my notes and set to memory phrases written about her—*tireless activist, reformist, fighter, persuasive,* and *in a class by herself.* I couldn't wait to meet Louise B. Raggio, the woman behind these identifications.

Louise Raggio

As she walked down the stairs, her proud posture and spunky step exuded an air of purpose. She was direct and unquestionably passionate about her belief systems as we talked on the way to her office. Once there, Louise grabbed an afghan and took a seat in a recliner while I pulled up a chair. The corner plate glass windows slanted sunlight onto the plants clustered on the credenza as Louise jumped right into her tales.

Born in 1918 to Swedish and German parents, she grew up poor on a farm outside of Austin, Texas. As a child she helped on the farm, but her educationally supportive parents made sure she received schooling. From Austin High School she graduated as valedictorian, and from the University of Texas in Austin she graduated Phi Beta Kappa and held the number two spot in the class. She was the first woman to be awarded a Rockefeller

Foundation scholarship, which earned her a nine-month internship in Washington, D.C. In 1947 she entered the night law program at Southern Methodist University in Dallas and received her Doctor of Jurisprudence degree in 1952.

It took two years for Louise to find a job; however, U.S. District Court Judge Sarah T. Hughes influenced Henry Wade to hire his first female assistant, and Louise served in that role from 1954 to 1956. Under Mr. Wade, Louise became the first woman prosecutor in a Texas criminal court. Then in 1956 her husband, Grier Raggio, started his own law firm and she joined him. But she found herself frustrated by laws that treated married women like property and angered by the dismissive attitudes of state lawmakers. Fueled by these injustices, Louise embarked upon a journey that would earn her the label as the woman instrumental in changing the law on women's rights and families in Texas.

With her first major landmark—the Marital Property Act of 1967—she gained the reputation as a leading reformer in the nation. She went on to push two other family law acts through the legislature that helped to create the Texas Family Code. She then became the first woman elected to the board of directors of the State Bar of Texas and to serve as trustee of the Texas Bar Foundation.

For her efforts in women's rights, Louise has received a multitude of honors: Texas Women's Hall of Fame inductee, Margaret Brent Outstanding Woman Lawyer, State Bar of Texas Citation of Merit for Family Code, Dallas Bar Foundation Distinguished Career Award, Texas Trailblazer Award, and the Veteran Feminist of America Award.

And this veteran of women's rights is going strong at the age of eighty-two. Along with her three sons—Grier H. Jr., Thomas L., and Kenneth G.—and several other associates, the firm of Raggio & Raggio continues to fight for people. During the interview it was said that her mother, Hilma Matilda Ballerstedt, would have given the last drop of blood she had for Louise. This image of a mother willing to shed blood for her child obviously foreshadowed Louise Ballerstedt Raggio's role in the justice system.

Rose-Mary Rumbley

humorist; author

Amy Hass Brau

b. 1894

Now here's my mother's sexual education—one sentence when she took me to college. In the dormitory room we never said THE word, Mother just said, "Rose-Mary, you are alone for the first time in your life, now don't you dare get ruined." That was it.

Rose-Mary and mother, Amy Hass Brau, in downtown Dallas

MONEY WAS IMPORTANT to my mother. She was always conscious that at one time her family had money then lost it during the Depression. They lost their house and had to move into a smaller one, but I don't think that bothered her. No, I don't think she grieved. She wasn't an unhappy person after the Depression and the war because everybody went through it, but she was always conscious that at one time she had wealth then it was gone.

Losing the money made her dependent on my daddy, which was all right then, you see, so she grew up relying on the man. She loved Daddy and he took total care of her. He did everything. Mother believed you let your husband earn the living and you stayed home to rear the children, and she was satisfied with that.

But the worst thing you could ever be, according to Mother, was common. Now that is a Southern term, common, but she'd tell me not to be common and not to be uppity either. See you couldn't get to where you felt better than someone else. I can hear her say to me, "Watch it Rose-Mary, you're getting uppity. The higher you fly, the harder you're going to fall." You had to be right there in the middle with God and Mother.

I remember Mama said I was to get two things that would make me secure on this earth. She said, "Believe in God and get your teachers certificate." It was important I become a teacher so when my husband died I would be able to support myself. You see, that was something she could not do because she was reared a lady per se; she went to school, but still she thought only common women worked. But she said I could only teach school when my husband died, so it really upset her when I taught school and my husband was alive and we had children.

Mother did very little with her hands. She didn't work; she just had a good time, see, no crafts, no cooking, no sewing. She just hated house cleaning, and Daddy did the yard work. No, Mother had a diamond on every finger. I'm serious. There were a few things left from the riches, but she had the diamonds, and at the end of her life she put on every piece of jewelry she owned. That was the only eccentric thing she did, adding a diamond to each finger as she got older.

I think Mother would have loved to have been an actress, but she was resigned to the fact that she was my mother. She loved the movies, and I remember that is the only time she'd leave me. She'd leave me with Daddy some nights and go to the movies by herself, then she'd come home so moved by some film. I remember one time she came home and said, "Oh, I have just seen *Shepherd of the Hills*. It was such a moving picture. I was so touched by it that I just don't think I can fix dinner."

I think you could say Mama was interesting. Her strength had to be her stamina to go and do things. When I'd pick her up to take her to my speeches, she'd literally run out of her home. She never learned to drive, you see, she was either chauffeured or rode the bus. She was independent in that respect, and she was feisty and never became feeble.

And she jogged and, yes, my mother loved to walk. She started walking for her health because she was not well after I was born since I was such a late baby. The doctor told her she needed to walk every day, so Daddy marked off one, two, and three miles for her, and all the kids in the neighborhood would go walking with her. That was when I was little, but it really paid off because she was walking just the week before she got sick and died at the age of ninety.

She loved to go to parties. Now she never entertained a lot, never played bridge or cards, but she loved teas and parties, and I took her to every one of them. Oh, and she loved the United Daughters of the Confederacy. And she believed in God and was a devout Christian. She believed that everything was born in you. And if people did anything good, she'd say, "Isn't that wonderful, they were born that way." And if they did anything bad, she'd say, "How sad to be born that way." You know, I can hear her voice even now.

I could always depend on her being there when I came home from school, and one of my fondest memories is when I'd get home and she'd sit down and pull her ears forward and say, "I'm all ears, tell me everything." So I'd sit down and tell her and we'd just sit and rock. We never sat still, and my daddy would say, "You know, you need to be connected to something. You could run the washer with all that rocking."

> *. . . one of my fondest memories is when I'd get home and she'd sit down and pull her ears forward and say, "I'm all ears, tell me everything."*

She did a lot with me. I was an only child and my parents were quite elderly when I was born—they were in their forties—but age didn't matter. I was her little star at all times. Mother made sure that at age three I took expression lessons and gave little readings to Sunday school classes or anybody who would listen. She enrolled me in all those classes. She believed you had to have expression lessons to be brought out, and it was very essential to Mama that I be brought out.

She loved to go to my recitals, you see. She just loved those and was always on the front row encouraging me. She would just always tell me, "You were fine. You were wonderful." And she'd tell me that if I did the best I could, then that's all I could do. She was so gentle and supportive.

You know, what I miss most about Mother is her telling all these Dallas stories over and over and over again. She would talk about when she was a little girl, and she would just tell stories—school stories, downtown Dallas stories, stories about the first gas pipeline. She saw the first car in Dallas, the first motion picture in Dallas, and she saw vaudeville. Oh, she was so proud she lived in Dallas. But Mother never wrote these stories down, no, she was just out for a party. So I've written them down and had them published, but she never lived to see the first of my three books published. And all three are on Dallas, and they're all big Mama books.

I am very much turning into my mother. I guess one of the first times I realized this was when I noticed that I started speaking to everybody on the street. You see, Mother loved to talk to everybody. And so I am becoming my mother.

One evening, when my children were in elementary school, I reminded them of the covered dish supper at the church. "Granny is bringing a pie," I announced. They both had surprised looks on their faces. "Can Granny bake a pie?" my daughter questioned.

My kids had never seen my mother in the kitchen. Mom managed to cook enough when I was growing up to keep me healthy, but she really preferred the department store to the stove. I assured my daughter that Granny was perfectly able to BUY a pie from the baker. Mother taught me how to shop—not cook!

I did cook for my family, but when the last kid left, I blew out the pilot light!

Rose-Mary Rumbley

This was my second interview of the day, so I was afraid I would have trouble switching gears. Since there was a break of about thirty minutes before Rose-Mary Rumbley was to arrive, I spent time putting files in order and thumbing through a magazine I'd picked up off the coffee table. But the little bit of trepidation I felt about being on top of things for this next meeting was for naught, because the minute the door opened and Rose-Mary walked in, I knew she'd keep me hopping. She was the very picture of ebullience with chin-length blonde hair that bounced with each step, matched only by the buoyancy in her voice. It only took a nanosecond to deduce that Rose-Mary is a spitfire of a woman whose animated personality held promise of an interesting session. And interesting it was.

I soon learned that the place where we were to conduct the interview was not going to be available, and since I was in unfamiliar territory I accepted Rose-Mary's offer to find us a quiet spot. That's when the adventure began. Since she is a firm believer in fitness, she suggested I gather the things I needed so we could walk to a nearby restaurant. I did as she said and off we went. The restaurant was a couple of blocks away, but we covered the distance in record pace—both in walking distance and in talking speed. You see, Rose-Mary Rumbley can spin a yarn with rapid-fire speed.

We arrived at this wonderfully quaint café, only to learn they weren't open to the public yet. So in her never-say-die fashion, Rose-Mary didn't miss a beat in deciding on an alternative site and off we walked, and walked and walked. Finally we arrived at the local health club and took the elevator up to the gym floor where we found a table off to one side to carry on the interview amid blaring disco music and periodic nasal announcements. But Rose-Mary wasn't fazed as she bubbled over with tales of her mama.

Rose-Mary is a Dallas gem. She is reputed to be Dallas' most sought-after speaker as she is known for her entertaining and unique brand of humor. Part and parcel to her love of being before the public is her experience with acting. She appeared in the movie *Paper Moon* with Tatum and Ryan O'Neal and in several television productions. She has also acted in supporting roles with John Davidson, Ginger Rogers, Van Johnson, and Ruta Lee.

Rose-Mary has authored three books: *A Century of Class: The Unauthorized History of Dallas*; *Dallas, Too* (all humorous stories of her native city); and *What, No Chili?* (a children's book about Texas festivals). She has written two plays: *Queen Mollie,* the story of Mollie Bailey of circus fame, and *Trail of Honor,* a story of Sam Houston. She also writes weekly columns for two Dallas publications. A historian, Dr. Rumbley thoroughly researches the information she uses in her presentations.

I can only imagine that when Dr. Rose-Mary Rumbley stands before a group of people to talk about her mama and those Dallas

Rose-Mary Rumbley

stories she so loves, the words flow freely and easily. And I can only imagine that somewhere her mama is smiling at her daughter, Rose-Mary Rumbley, for keeping the stories alive.

Sonja Eva Singletary

professor of surgery, department of oncology,
University of Texas M. D. Anderson Cancer Center

Eva Singletary and mother, Agnes Singletary, 1995

Agnes Küll Singletary

b. 1919

*Mother's soul is a strong wind blowing. One of my favorite times as a kid
was right before a big storm. Usually Mother would have to come get me to
go back inside, but I liked the feel of the air starting to blow and the power
of that. So I think that is how I see her.*

M Y MOTHER IS A STRONG, DETERMINED WOMAN, and the best place
to start is actually the beginning of her story when she first came to
the United States. She met my father during WW II, and when he came
back he brought her over to marry her. But what is interesting about that is

Agnes Küll Singletary, Germany, 1945

Agnes Singletary

she grew up in the capital city of Estonia, and my father lived in a rural area of South Carolina, so it was quite a difference to come over to a rural area with dirt roads and wooden houses. Now it was anticipated my father would marry the preacher's daughter when he got back from the war, so Mother didn't exactly get met with a welcoming party.

I don't think it bothered her that people considered her a foreigner, but I was impressed with how she adapted to this situation. She got involved in community events—the church, the 4-H Club, the garden club—and wasn't going to let anything deter her. So it is the word pioneer that comes to mind because my mother was willing to try new things even though she wasn't in the ideal setting.

Growing up on the farm you learned the philosophy that there was something everyone could do to help out, and Mom helped out, so I wouldn't consider her just someone in the home. She worked out in the fields because it was a family farm, and that was the system where one farm helped another. I can see her working out in the fields—picking cotton, planting tobacco.

I believe that hardship on the farm would usually have to do with financial problems, so there would be times she was worried about having food on the table. But somehow she managed. We had a family garden, and she'd just make ends meet. I can see her in that garden, bent over with a bandanna on her head and a bucket in her hand. I think she wished for fewer hard times, but overall I don't think she regrets living on the farm.

You know Mom is an artist. In my mind I always see her with paint on her clothes and again wearing a bandanna. But Mom became an art teacher, I think, one for economic reasons and two because she thought she could do it. She got her certificate because they were bringing art into the classroom. During the summer I would be her assistant, and I remember how all the little kids would run out and hug her. I have a lot of her artwork at my home, but I don't think I have one favorite piece. She did a bit of everything, and that's kind of her deal not to stay in one niche; instead she tried different things—ceramics, copper jewelry, making tables with tile, stained glass—and my dad provided the paraphernalia for each project. My parents had a strong relationship, and that became more noticeable to me after I left home and would go back and see the two of them working together. Even though my father was not interested in the arts per se, he would always be with her.

Another side to Mom is her competitiveness. Once she was in a cooking contest. She was selected as one of the best chicken cookers in South Carolina, and back then that was a real honor. And she had all of us kids involved in different 4-H projects, so we always competed in the county fair. But she didn't push us. Part of it was just an expectation that you didn't sit idle. It was just assumed you were going to be involved, and if you did, well then fine, and if you didn't, it wasn't a big deal. I remember one of my 4-H responsibilities was raising

Agnes Singletary, 3rd place winner— South Carolina Chicken Cooking Contest; Clemson, South Carolina; recipe: "Chicken For All," August 1963

Agnes Küll Singletary, 1993

chickens, and she told me they would be better egg layers if I read to them. So after school I would go read to the chickens. You know I swallowed the whole thing, since of course what she was doing was making me read.

You can't get much by Mom because of what she calls her radar. One thing that comes to mind about that is once when one of us kids took some candy from the grocery store. Mother caught on and made us all take it back, and the huge man who worked there looked like he could eat us in one swallow. So it was impressed on us that one should never take anything that doesn't belong to them. Mother made her point.

Mom is the family disciplinarian. You could tell when she was displeased because she would verbally let you know that she thought it was wrong. Growing up I can't remember a time she spanked us. But she would threaten us with a switch and we'd have to go pick out our own. Then she'd just brandish it around and barely touch our legs with it, so it was just the whole thing of having to pick out the switch.

I would definitely thank Mom not only for teaching me to be honest but for trusting me enough to let me do my own thing. She would never interfere. No, she would just ask if things were okay and then offer suggestions, but she wouldn't interfere. My mother wasn't surprised I went into medicine. She wasn't against it, but I could tell that both parents were concerned because not many women were going into medicine at that time. But they gave me the freedom to do what I wanted.

Mom has her feet on the ground and is able to see the bigger picture, and I think her advice has certainly stood the test of time. I remember once she was visiting me, and I woke late one morning and went into this litany of stuff I had to do that day. She told me I looked tired and needed my rest, then she said, "And let me remind you, young lady, that the walls of M. D. Anderson were standing before you got here, and they'll be standing after you leave. You do not have to think you're the only one who will hold them up." I remind myself of that constantly. What it taught me in terms of leadership is it's important not to consider yourself the only person who can run the show.

But Mom also has a private side. I remember one time after President Kennedy was assassinated, I was alone with my mother when he was being buried. Mother and I were watching the funeral procession on TV, and I remember how upset she was. I was surprised to see her that way because she had always been so strong, so I couldn't understand it. I was playing on the floor, and I remember where she was sitting in the den in one of those rocking chairs. She was just so silent. And that was a special time, a private time together with Mom.

You know, after I have visited my Mom, we always cry when I leave. It is just so hard.

Estonian Hamburger

> 2 lbs. ground beef
> ¾ c. bread crumbs or mashed potatoes
> 1 or 2 eggs
> 1¼ c. milk or heavy cream
> 1 Tbsp. minced onion
> 1 tsp. salt
> ½ tsp. pepper
> Bread crumbs and butter for frying

Soak the bread crumbs in the milk or cream. Season ground beef with salt and pepper, and mix well. Add egg(s), minced onion, and soaked bread crumbs or mashed potatoes to meat; mix well. Set mixture on a wet board. Roll it into a thick sausage, even in size throughout, and divide into equal portions. Using wet hands, shape the portions into patties. Coat the patties with bread crumbs and fry in hot butter.

Estonian Sugar Cake

> 4 eggs
> 1⅓ c. sugar
> Grated peel or juice from ½ lemon
> ⅔ c. half & half
> 1½ c. flour
> ¾ lb. butter or margarine

2 tsp. baking powder
I tsp. vanilla

Cream eggs with sugar. Add lemon peel or juice. Combine flour with baking powder and add to creamed mixture. Melt butter or margarine, and add it along with the half & half to cake batter. Mix thoroughly. Bake at 350 degrees for 50 minutes. Use a pan that is slightly larger than two quarts for baking.

Chicken for All

2 lb. chicken
2 tsp. salt
6 Tbsp. shortening
2 c. raw rice
I bell pepper
I onion
6 oz. olives
I no. 2 can tomatoes
I no. 2 can garden peas
⅛ lb. butter or margarine
I can any standard brand beer or 2 c. water

Make standard cuts of chicken. Roll in flour with salt added. Heat shortening in skillet: fry chicken until light brown. Remove chicken to oven pot. Add 2 cups raw rice over chicken. Cut bell pepper and onion into small pieces and add to skillet with ⅛ pound margarine or butter. Brown lightly. Add peas, olives, and tomatoes (drained) and mix. Pour over chicken and rice one can of beer or water. Cook for I hour at 375 degrees. Yield: 6 servings.

Sonja Eva Singletary

In a microcosmic community in the metropolitan city of Houston resides the Medical Center. Buildings rising skyward in stair-step heights border upon each other forming a honeycomb for healing. As you enter this world, you feel the synergy created by the women and men who unite their efforts to find cures and relief for those suffering from illness or disease. And in this environment you will find Dr. Sonja Eva Singletary.

Once inside the University of Texas M. D. Anderson Cancer Center, I took the elevator to the tenth floor. During the ascent I recalled the days ten years ago I had spent at this site with my mother before she lost her battle to cancer. A bit shaken, I was glad when the door opened and I was not met by anyone. So I took a deep breath then turned and walked to Dr. Eva Singletary's office. Eva's handshake was gentle and her eyes warm and compassionate, and both spoke stories about this beautifully perceptive and tenderhearted woman who, over the course of several hours, would laugh, reminisce, and cry about life with her mother.

Dr. S. Eva Singletary
Photo courtesy of Karen Barfield, Barfield Photography, Houston, Texas

Sonja Eva Singletary was born and reared on a farm in Coward, South Carolina. It was in junior high school she decided to become a medical doctor. Then as a young medical student she chose to specialize in cancer, basing her decision on the fact that at the time one of the only options for cancer treatment was surgery. Since then she has played a significant role in the progress of treatment, early detection, and prevention of this disease.

In 1985 Dr. Singletary was asked to join the M. D. Anderson staff after completing a two-year surgical oncology fellowship at the cancer center. Two years later she was named Chief of the Melanoma Section and in 1990 became Chief of the Surgical Breast Section.

Dr. Singletary is a nationally acknowledged surgeon and advocate for breast cancer awareness and has devoted her career to caring for women with breast cancer. Her reputation as one of the premier breast surgeons in Texas and the United States keeps Houston and M. D. Anderson at the forefront as a world-renowned medical center. However, her knowledge and expertise go beyond patient care and to the young women and men who are tomorrow's doctors and medical educators as she is also a professor of surgery at M. D. Anderson.

Dr. Singletary's public education efforts to prevent breast cancer are numerous. She coordinated the development of "Choices: Breast Cancer Treatment Options," an innovative interactive computer program for patients. She also joined the San Jacinto Girl Scouts in developing and promoting "In the Pink," a breast cancer awareness interest project for girls ages eleven to seventeen. For Dr. Singletary's outstanding contributions she was named to the Texas Women's Hall of Fame, recognized with the Business and Professional Women's Club Award and the Texas Executive Women "Women on the Move" Award, and in 1999 received the Cancer Fighters Eagle Award.

While there is so much more to her accomplishments, suffice it to say that just as she sees her mother's soul as a strong wind blowing, I believe that same description applies to the very soul of Dr. Sonja Eva Singletary as well.

Bert Kruger Smith

Hogg Foundation consultant; author

Fania Feldman Kruger and Bert Kruger Smith

Fania Feldman Kruger

b. 1892

Mother said she was not very religious, but I think she had a great feeling
for humanity and a great wish to be remembered. She believed in being kind
to people, and she was very much an advocate for the underdog.

I HAVE TWO FOND AND STRONG MEMORIES of Mother's hands. In one her hands are on the typewriter as she is doing poetry, and in the other her hands are in this thin strudel dough. So those are two ways I think of her using her hands, and they showed parts of her that were different.

217

My mother was a writer, and I always saw her hands in that image. Whenever I saw her at that typewriter, there was a kind of awe, a wonderment at what she was doing. And sometimes when I walked into the bedroom and found her writing, I guess I wished she would play with me instead of always writing. I would try not to disturb her, but sometimes I did.

She had a big desk near the window at the end of her bedroom. She'd have typing paper boxes full of poems and things she had written and rewritten on the desk, and that is where her material went. She worked and typed and wrote daily. She just pursued her writing quietly, and I don't think most people knew about it until she was married, had a home, then had the time. Mother wrote and was published in national magazines, was in the Institute of Letters, and won awards. She apparently was a well-known minor poet who was invited different places from time to time to talk and read works.

Fania Feldman Kruger

In Wichita Falls she joined a group of women who wrote. They would meet on Saturdays to read and discuss their work, and Mother invited me to go. I must have been an adolescent at the time that I joined that group, and we were all trying to write. This was where Mother was most involved with me, not in the cooking, in the writing. She was very definite in wanting if not perfection something close to it. She was always working on her poetry, always writing, and she was always concerned about whether it was good enough. She would critique my work, sometimes more critically than I would have liked, but then she would compliment me. Sometimes she'd read her poetry to us, not often, but the women in the group were very accepting and I think very appreciative of her skill and her being published because it was a type of proof she was a professional.

One of my strongest memories of a mother and daughter thing was going to the writer's conference in Colorado with her. At the time I was eleven or twelve, and we'd get a room at a boardinghouse and be there for the summer. She and I would take some classes or meet with some professors, and we'd do this summer after summer because Wichita Falls was so hot and my father would send us off where it was cool. I just thought, as children do, that this was the way life was. You know, you always think that other families are like your own. I believe that if I could thank her for one thing, I think it would be for the spirit she gave me for writing and doing for others.

Fania Feldman Kruger

I saw a lot of love in my family. Mother and Dad were very demonstrative, very loving toward one another, and they had a caring marriage and weren't bashful about showing affection. Dad would kiss her and stroke her hair. Some of my favorite lines in a poem titled "Against My Going" that Mother wrote to my father read, "Your love will fill my heart to overflowing/ Your eyes will light the way I shall be going." And I think that is such a statement of her feelings for my father.

The other image of her hands, like I said, was when she made strudel. I don't think she wore an apron, no, I think she just stood there rolling out the dough and getting the things ready. She was very confident—like an army general—when she made the strudel; she knew exactly what she was doing, and she did it well. Mother was very much a perfectionist, and her standards were not matched by anybody else. So her strudel was just marvelous, and she became very well known for it. When I went to work for the University of Texas in Austin, she'd send platters of it up to the office, and people just adored it. But there was not a single time she invited me to come learn to make the strudel.

Mother wasn't an open, talkative woman. No, she was pretty much reserved, and she was just like a steel rod. You didn't know it when you first met her, but she had her convictions. We were the only house, I bet, in Wichita Falls where the colored people came to the front door. You've got to remember that wasn't done in those times when everything was segregated, yet Mother was very favorably regarded by the townspeople. She wasn't pushy with her ideas; she was this soft-spoken, gentle, un-pushy kind of person, and she just had the strength of a steel rod in her.

One time she was invited to Marshall, Texas, to give a lecture. When she got to the hotel, some women told her not to speak at the Negro college because she was a white woman. But she was absolutely unwilling to cancel her engagement and went out and

Fania Feldman Kruger

gave the speech, which you wouldn't have expected of this very seemingly timid woman, but she did it.

Mother had two sayings that I can recall. One was a Yiddish expression that meant "everything in measure." She believed things should be done in measure and at the right time. The other I remember her telling me was simply "Don't." She did have this interesting sense of humor. But she was single-minded and really wasn't the playing kind of mother, so I always think of her as being a grown woman and never think of her as young. Mother was proper, very proper, and always dressed even for breakfast. Mother was just very gracious, very proper. I guess strong would be another word I associate with Mother, and another would be loving, really loving. We could go down the street and if we saw a child, she'd stop and pat him and talk to him. She was very loving in that way.

One of Mother's most positive qualities was she had a tremendous push for achievement, and she taught me that by example. When Mother first got to Fort Worth she was fifteen, and the only job she could get was carrying barrels in a liquor store. She was Russian and had to learn English, so she went to night school immediately and learned to write and speak a beautiful English, which was even more remarkable because it wasn't her native language.

I think she showed a lot of strength when my father was quite ill. She really took over. She hadn't driven for years, but when he had his leg amputated she learned to drive again and really helped out in the family jewelry store. Shortly after Dad died in 1952, she moved to Austin and rented an apartment near the university. Everybody at the school knew her because she would walk to the campus day after day even though she had arthritis pretty bad. She had been so hungry all those years for learning and schooling that when she got to Austin, it was like a starving child finding a feast.

People just loved to talk and listen to Mother. She had a musical voice, a quiet voice, and people adored it. Mother was just bigger than life.

Strudel

Dough:
>   1 box Swansdown cake flour
>   9 eggs, dropped in well of flour
>   Orange juice, several spoons
>   1½ c. Wesson oil
>   1 c. sugar
>   Grated orange rind
>   Grated lemon rind
>   1 tsp. almond extract
>   1 tsp. vanilla

Filling:
>   4 oz. shredded coconut
>   12 oz. pecans (broken up)
>   1 lb. dates (cut up)
>   48 oz. cherry preserves
>   20 oz. orange marmalade
>   Grated rind of 2 oranges, 2 lemons
>   1 tsp. almond flavoring
>   1 tsp. vanilla flavoring
>   Sugar and cinnamon, several spoons

Mix dough, leaving out portion of flour, then put dough in flour and mix until possible to roll. Cut the dough in four parts and roll out each part. Put filling in dough. Cut through and shape back into a roll. Spread top of dough with Wesson oil and sprinkle with sugar and cinnamon. Bake in 350-degree oven until done.

Spiced Coffee Cake

>   2 c. flour
>   ½ tsp. salt
>   2 tsp. baking powder
>   1 c. sugar
>   1½ tsp. cinnamon
>   ¼ tsp. nutmeg
>   ½ tsp. cloves
>   ½ c. shortening
>   1 well-beaten egg
>   2 Tbsp. dark molasses

¾ c. milk

Sift flour, salt, baking powder, sugar, and spices. Cut in shortening until mixture resembles coarse crumbs. Reserve ½ cup of this mixture. Add egg, molasses, and milk to rest. Mix lightly. Pour into wax paper lined 8-inch square pan. Top with reserved mixture. Sprinkle with ½ cup chopped walnuts. Bake in 375 degree oven for 40 minutes.

Bert Kruger Smith

Bert and Sid Smith's home offers a treetop view out windows running along its back wall. Built atop a hill, its panoramic stretch invites the imaginings of a lark soaring above the earth's terrain, and that is just how I felt once I began the interview—like a lark transported into the life of Bert Kruger Smith.

Once Bert settled onto one sofa, I noted the sunlight created a silken backdrop against her poised body. Sid, her husband, bustled about trying not to join her, but that was futile as they appeared interwoven in life stories. Needless to say, he took his place on the nearby sofa and, like her aficionado, remained by her side talking every now and then, nodding to affirm fond recollections, and laughing at curious life moments. And throughout the interview, the love, respect, and familiarity between Bert and Sid filled the space so that by the time I left, I felt I had known them forever.

Bert, a gracious woman with a refined, cosmopolitan demeanor, proved a kaleidoscope of surprises. While soft in speech she was also hearty in laughter; while firm in expectations she was also soft with compassion. And so it stands that her life work reflects her soul. And for much of that life work, she served as special consultant to the Hogg Foundation for Mental Health at the University of Texas in Austin.

Bert's work has been driven by the very compassion she houses. Her involvement with over one hundred memberships,

Bert Kruger Smith

boards, and committees runs the gamut: adult services, groups for the elderly, ethics, health care, children with learning disabilities, mental health, nursing homes, problems of the handicapped, and social welfare.

And for this woman, who much like her mother has a steel rod strengthening her beliefs, the honors and awards have been justifiably awarded by various groups—Jewish Family Services, Family Eldercare, Women in Communications, Texas Women's Hall of Fame, Texas Association for Retarded Citizens, and the National Conference of Christians and Jews.

Nevertheless, Bert's contributions continue. She has written seven books, forty articles, thirty-four pamphlets, and four leaflets. As well, she has co-authored or edited seven introductions and afterwords for books and seven scripts for film and multimedia. She has hosted a series of thirty-nine half-hour radio interviews, and has conducted seminars, workshops, and lectures in the mental health area.

For her dedication, Bert has been tapped by sources that would reap the benefits of her knowledge and insight for special assignments. To name a few the list includes: Texas delegate to Washington, D.C., for "Speak Out USA!"; reporter on self-help survey findings at the World Federation for Mental Health meeting; presenter of testimony at the attorney general's public hearing on nursing homes in 1978, and of testimony on support systems for the elderly to the President's Commission on Mental Health in 1977.

In view of all Bert has contributed to society, it is understandable that the descriptions of her mother, Fania Feldman Kruger, as an advocate, a writer, a woman of strength and love, and a steel rod are but parcels in the character passed along to her daughter, Bert Kruger Smith.

Carolyn T. Sumners

director of astronomy, Houston Museum of
Natural Science

Carolyn Sumners and mother, Eunice Kenney Taylor, February 2000

Margaret Eunice Kenney Taylor

b. 1917

*There's just never been life without Mother. She is by far the biggest
influence in my life because, you know, the person who builds the pen in
which you bounce is certainly important.*

MY MOTHER'S FAMILY lived on a farm, and she remembers listening to the car radio because they had no electricity in the house. But she talks about how they had everything they needed on this farm. And, this is a cool story, she remembers sitting on the steps of the courthouse with a bunch of kids listening to the Cross of Gold speech of William Jennings Bryant during the Scopes trial.

You see Mother is a matriarch of every environment and definitely a matriarch who thought education was important. Now I think a matriarch isn't a beloved mother of a tribe but is the one who says what is important and administers tough love and the one to whom everybody traces their expectations. Mother had a college degree in mathematics and was head of the math department for thirty-five years at this school in Tennessee, and she wanted the kids to not be emotionally dependent on her. She was looking at how they needed math to succeed and survive, so she always wanted the seniors to be accountable to her ideals—not that she was conditional but that she thought there were some things you couldn't expect a matriarch to put up with. Now a matriarch may not always be right, but she's always powerful, and Mother didn't cut the kids any slack. She demanded a lot of them. Mother believes you give people respect by raising expectations not by lowering standards, and she taught people to value what they could do.

And she always demanded a lot of me. I remember when I was quite the chatterbox in elementary school—I think I was in fifth grade—and Mother would send math books to the teacher and tell her to slap a page in front of

Carolyn Sumners and Eunice Kenney Taylor

me when I opened my mouth. So whenever I was a discipline problem I didn't get punished, I just got more math to work. But I didn't mind because I loved math.

> *. . . her legacy is . . . her appreciation and respect for life, her sense of adventure. It is her strong, positive presence.*

Mom's relationships were always minds-on, not necessarily hands-on. So in dealing with her, you had to know where her head was. You had to know what she was thinking, what she wanted. So you never focused on the emotion because the idea that she was emotionally there for you wasn't as important as she was mentally there for you. Mother does what she does because she loves you. You know, it's much easier to not care, so once you buy into that, you understand it is the good of you she cares about. When I look at these young ones today who have no parent really present in their lives, it makes me sad. So what having a mother like mine did is it didn't cause me to have any questions. I knew I had been designated as special and that one of the greatest gifts Mom has given me is my absolute, unfailing identity.

It's interesting, but it never occurred to Mom that there was any discrimination between men and women. She remembers traveling around the country during WW II, teaching airplane identification to pilots, and she never acts like this was anything special just because she was a woman. I know it never occurred to me that my being hired at the age of twenty-two to run the planetarium was unusual, and that never would have occurred to my mom because she believes there are no expectations related to being female.

With her you know life is real. I never was taught that life was fair or that the playing field was even. I was taught that it was tilted and usually away from me. It wasn't that anyone was out to get you, it was just that life was not a debatable thing. If you do something wrong, you don't package it and make excuses for it, you try to not let it happen again. Now Mom is opinionated. For her most of life is black and white, and there are huge levels of expectation. Morals are important, and what is right and wrong is absolute.

And she is determined. If something is to be done and she believes in it, then it'll be done. I mean, if you're going to go on a trip, then you're going to do it. If you're going to go to college and make good grades, then it will happen. She is just realistic about life and says you should always look for adventure because you can always have that.

Mom's soul is large and dominating, yet she's positive and fun loving, there's no doubt about that. She is just so full of life and feels life is something to be lived and not to get tangled up in emotionally. She believes that if you're depressed, then you go to work or do something. It is the idea that if you have anything causing you a problem, you simply replace the problem. She believes these thoughts are just trapped in your head, so you have to break the loop. She's so very pragmatic.

I think her legacy is definitely a huge footprint for my kids, one they don't even recognize yet. I mean, it is the years she has spent with them, the standards and concepts of right and wrong, and the tolerance of older people. It is her appreciation and respect for life, her sense of adventure. It is her strong, positive presence.

Corn Pudding

3 eggs
I c. milk
I Tbsp. sugar
2 Tbsp. butter
I tsp. salt
2 c. cream style corn (I can)
2 Tbsp. flour
I Tbsp. finely chopped onion
2 Tbsp. Lipton chicken cup-o-soup

Beat eggs. Add milk, salt, and sugar. Mix corn with other ingredients. Pour into greased casserole. Bake at 350 degrees uncovered for I hour.

Squash Delight Casserole

I lb. squash
I tsp. sugar
½ c. mayonnaise
½ c. chopped onion

¼ c. chopped green pepper
½ c. chopped pecans
I egg
½ c. grated cheese
½ c. chopped pimiento
½ stick butter
I c. bread crumbs
Salt and pepper

Cook squash, which has been diced. Drain, add butter, and mash. Add other ingredients and put in a casserole. Bake for 40 minutes at 350 degrees.

Pineapple Casserole

This is the recipe people want when I take a dish to a luncheon. It is good with ham.

I can pineapple chunks
½ c. shredded mild cheddar cheese
3 tsp. flour
½ stick butter or margarine
½ c. sugar

Drain pineapple and reserve juice. Melt butter. Stir in flour and sugar. Add pineapple juice and thicken into a sauce. Layer pineapple chunks and cheese, pour sauce over layers. Top with crushed Ritz crackers and dot with butter. Bake in 350-degree oven for 25 minutes.

Southern Pecan Pie

4 eggs
I ¼ c. cane syrup
I ½ c. broken pecan meats
I c. sugar
4 Tbsp. butter
I tsp. vanilla

Boil sugar and syrup together for three minutes. Beat eggs, pour slowly into hot syrup, add butter, vanilla, and pecan meats. Pour into uncooked pie shell and bake in 350-degree oven for 45 minutes.

Marshmallow Brownies

2 squares unsweetened chocolate
2 sticks margarine
4 eggs
2 c. sugar
1½ c. flour
1 tsp. baking powder
1 c. broken nut meats
2 tsp. vanilla

Melt chocolate and margarine. Beat eggs, add sugar, then add all other ingredients and the chocolate mixture. Spread in greased 11 x 13-inch pan and bake at 325 degrees for 35 minutes.

Topping for Marshmallow Brownies

Melt 1 stick of margarine, 2 squares of unsweetened chocolate, 1 small can evaporated milk, and 1 cup sugar. Beat in 1 box confectioner's sugar. The mixture will be thin. As soon as the cake is done, cover with a 6-ounce bag of miniature marshmallows. Then pour on hot icing. When cool cut in 1-inch squares.

Carolyn T. Sumners

Walking into the Houston Museum of Natural Science, I found the interior alive with the youthful voices of starry-eyed children surrounded by items from the past, present, and future. Their exuberance infected my spirits as I entered the Burke Baker Planetarium to experience a journey into the "Passages of Time," the latest production written and directed by my next interviewee—Dr. Carolyn T. Sumners, Director of Astronomy and the Physical Sciences at the museum for nearly thirty years.

Within seconds my excitement gave way to peacefulness brought on by the delicate sounds of music and the wispy clouds moving silently across the blue heavens painted on the domed ceiling. Then I turned my attention to the docent's explanations about the show, and when the lights went low, I watched as the universe began with the Big Bang and moved forward over a period of fifteen billion years to what we know it as today.

After I left the solitude of the darkened planetarium, I ran headfirst into my own Big Bang—Carolyn Sumners. This bright-eyed woman moves and talks at the speed of light, propelled by a frontiering spirit, bolstered with academic competency. Within seconds she drew me into her vision, into her world without boundaries. And at the heart of that world lies her mother, Margaret Eunice Kenney Taylor, an Irish woman with fire in her soul.

Carolyn is indeed her mother's daughter. Ever diligent, she graduated with high honors from both Vanderbilt University and the University of Houston and began a venture into the field of science education that has served her well.

Carolyn Sumners, February 2000

For twenty-nine years Carolyn has overseen the Burke Baker Planetarium and directed development of the Brown Solar Observatory and Earth Forum environmental simulator. In 1988 Dr. Sumners created the Challenger Learning Center problem-solving simulator, which has now been replicated in over thirty museum and science centers. In 1998 she directed the opening of the first full-view immersive large format video theater, Sky Vision, in the planetarium, and it will be replicated in ten planetariums and theaters in 2000.

In keeping with her inexhaustible nature, Carolyn is also curator for three permanent museum exhibit halls. She directs the museum's technology summer program with one hundred twenty science camps yearly along with classes for children, families, teachers, and adults.

Carolyn Sumners is also co-principal investigator on two grants, both of which are NASA-funded public outreach programs through Rice University. She also instructs all space shuttle astronauts in navigational star identification and is project director for the Toys in Space Program at the Johnson Space Center. This accomplished scientist produces two yearly satellite television broadcasts and regularly appears on Houston radio and television as an astronomy expert. Carolyn's frontier also traverses the world of writing with a science textbook series, *Science Discovery Works*, planetarium programs, adult nonfiction science books, and teachers' guides.

Her propensity for investigation, analysis, visualization, and conceptualization lies at the basis of the many awards Carolyn has received. Recognitions for her roles in the science fields include: Outstanding Houston Woman in Science by the YWCA, 1988; Federation of Business Women, 1989; Long Dedicated Service to the Profession from the Clear Lake Council of Technical Societies, 1994; and the Metropolitan Association for Teachers of Science, 1996.

And there you have her, Dr. Carolyn T. Sumners, a.k.a. the Big Bang, a woman in love with curiosity and science whose matriarch laid a solid foundation beneath her daughter's feet to allow the universe to become her frontier.

Betty Switzer

managing director of community development and rural services, Texas Commission on the Arts

Betty Switzer and Lillian Williamson

Lillian Ruth Brannon Williamson

b. 1910

Mother pretty well taught me I could do anything if I wanted it badly enough, and she taught me that through modeling rather than just talking about it.

I have lots of images of my mother's hands. I remember sitting in the Broadway Baptist Church in downtown Fort Worth as a little girl of maybe six or seven and looking at her hands. I would feel so secure just sitting and holding or rubbing her hands. She had lots of brown spots, and I'd count and trace them and that would make me feel safe. I remember she often wore gloves, and I remember her squeezing lemons for fresh lemonade she made in the summer. And of course I remember when I had a cold how she would rub Vick's salve on my chest then pin a warm cloth to my pajamas so it would keep the vapors in.

You know my mother has never been one to say a lot of I love you's, but certainly her love was displayed in the things she did. To comfort me Mother would make hot cocoa with lots of marshmallows in it, and she would make homemade ice cream or bring me a bowl of store-bought ice cream topped with chocolate syrup. And when it snowed she'd make snow ice cream. She'd add milk and vanilla and sugar to the snow then mix it up in a slusher. And I vividly remember an incident in junior high when I had a date. I was dressed and waiting for my date, but he didn't come. So Mother picked up the phone and called his house to see what the problem was. She was told my date had received a call that I was sick, so he had taken another girl to the dance. I was heartbroken and I remember she comforted me. I think her ability to be loving and giving and to be seen as a sweet, caring person is a good description of Mother's soul.

But another picture of Mother is that she was a product of the Depression, so I think it's always important for her to feel secure. She has always tithed to her church but also has emphasized the importance of savings. I guess the phrase I heard a lot, "Don't waste a thing," was rooted in Mother's Depression upbringing, and that's still what she believes today. It's very much her nature to recycle everything—paper towels, aluminum foil, margarine tubs—and I imagine if we walked into the kitchen right now we'd find a paper towel behind the cutting board because she says you shouldn't wipe

Lillian Ruth Brannon

your hands on a paper towel just once then throw it away.

She has a philosophy that if you're going to do something, then it has to be done right. I remember on Saturday mornings when we cleaned house we would have checks, and if anything was missed, we'd have to do it again. From that I learned you can't slop your way through things, and if you do something right the first time, it's not going to take as long to do it again. Those were big lessons I see myself applying today.

When I was young Daddy bought this grocery store, and we moved to the country. But it wasn't Mother's favorite thing. This was his dream and she just went along with it. He wasn't making the kind of money he had when he worked in town, so Mother started working. Now my mother's parents, who had retired from farming, lived on one side of the store, and we lived on the other. So when Mother started working, my grandmother became my other caregiver, and I had both women as positive forces in my life.

Lillian Ruth Brannon Williamson, 1949

Mother had stayed home with my sister and brother, but when I was nine years old she became a PBX operator at a bank. My dad was more of a dreamer than Mother since she was more pragmatic and rooted in the real world. And one thing Mother had was self-sufficiency. I think she was on the front edge of that because she was a goer, a doer, and in the 1950s I had lots of friends whose mothers were not nearly as active. You see even though she was in a marriage where she could have relied on my dad to do everything, she didn't. Well at that time I started working in the store sorting drink bottles, pricing items and putting them on the shelves, working in the fireworks stand, running the cash register, picking up produce, and pumping gas. While Mother was working I was getting a grounded value system from helping out at the store.

During that time I started school, and Mother decided I should be in a junior high in town as she believed that would give me a better educational foundation. So she and I moved to town and shared a home with an older lady. We'd go home to the country on Wednesday nights and weekends. Later when I got my driver's license, we moved back to the country, and I'd drive her to work and myself to school. You see she wanted me to have the things my friends had, and she worked hard to see that I did. To this day I attribute my time working in the store and my mother's support and determination for a good education as strong forces in giving me the self-confidence I have today.

One thing I remember most about Mother is she has always worked hard. She doesn't just sit down and do nothing. I can see her in the kitchen on Saturday nights, listening to the radio and ironing clothes. And after she started working, she would go to banking institutes to get credit hours, and she always maintained an active role in the church. Actually after she retired from the bank she started working part-time at the Lord's Supper Wax Display, first as a weekend docent then later as a full-time one. She did that for about fifteen years, so she's had two nice careers and has always kept her mind agile.

At this point I feel very much like I am on a caregiver level, but there are times when I also feel very much like her peer. When I talk about a situation with the children, she'll share how she had the same experiences with us. So Mother and I have this one-on-one conversation about how she confronted things. When we do that, we're sharing something we both understand, and that's when I most feel like her peer. I believe subconsciously that when my husband and I decided to move back to Fort Worth to help Mother, it was my way to give something back to her. I love her presence, so I make sure I tell her how much I appreciate all she has done for me and all she has given me.

I think Mother feels she's had a full life. I believe that when Daddy bought the store and moved us to the country, the move affected the life she had and the life she would have had, but I think she absolutely made the best of it.

At the interview's conclusion, Betty's mother sat with me and talked about her "famous" fried chicken. Following is her explanation of how she prepares it.

Fried Chicken

Fried chicken would generally be a Sunday lunch, and it would be served with cream potatoes, green beans, gravy, and sometimes brown-and-serve rolls and a salad, either a tossed salad or a congealed salad.

I usually buy a whole frying chicken and cut it up myself because I like the special side breasts, the center breasts, and the pully bone. And when you buy it at the grocery store you don't get those things.

So I cut it up and skin it and then put it in salt water because there's a certain amount of, I call it, slime underneath that skin. So I put it over in the salt water when I get it all cut up and skinned, then I take it out of the salt water and hold it under the faucet to wash off this slime.

Then I pat it dry and put it over in a container and cover it with sweet milk and soak it overnight—longer or a little less time if you want to.

Then I get a brown paper bag and put flour in that, and I drop as many pieces in as I think will coat without mixing in with each other. And I shake the pieces then lay them out on a piece of wax paper.

When I get my grease so hot it bubbles, I drop in enough pieces just to not crowd them, just enough to be in the bottom of the pan. I fry them in a deep, deep container rather than just a skillet because I steam it, and when you put that lid on, if it's not down in something deep, it could bubble up over on the stove. So I use more or less a Dutch oven. When they brown, I take them out and keep browning the other pieces in the deep fat.

The last pieces I fry are usually the more bony ones, then I put the other pieces I already fried back on top of those bony pieces and turn the fire to low and put the lid on. I let it steam in the grease for about thirty minutes. I found if I poured the grease off and put it in water, that all the coating came off and it wasn't as tasty. So I steam it in the grease that I fried it in. Of course, you need to watch your temperature.

But when you take it up you can cut it with a fork. It's just so tender and good.

Mo's Chocolate Dessert

I can still taste Mother's chocolate dessert. It is just drop-dead wonderful and creamy and light and delicious.

Cream together:
    2 sticks margarine
    1 lb. box powdered sugar
    3 heaping Tbsp. cocoa
Add:
    4 beaten egg yolks
    4 whites folded into above mixture
Mix:
    1 c. nuts

Pour mixture into graham cracker crust and top with some crumbs. Chill.

Unborn Fruit Cake

    1 small box graham crackers - roll fine
    1 box pitted dates - cut small
    ½ lb. candied cherries - whole
    14 marshmallows - cut small
    ¾ lb. pecans - chopped
    ½ pt. whipping cream - whip a little
    1 Tbsp. wine, whiskey, or rum

Mix thoroughly, adding cream only as needed to mold (should be real sticky). Pack back in wax-lined cracker box, tie firmly. Store in refrigerator.

Cherry Fruit Bake

    1 lb. butter
    2 c. sugar
    8 eggs
    4 c. flour
    2 tsp. baking powder
    ½ tsp. salt
    1 lb. candied cherries
    1 lb. candied pineapple
    1 lb. pecans
    2 oz. lemon extract

Cream butter, sugar, and eggs two at a time; beat well. Sift flour, baking powder, and salt together. Add part of flour to mixture then part of lemon extract. Roll cherries and pineapple in rest of flour and add to mixture, then add other ounce of lemon extract. Add pecans last. Pour in greased and floured pan. Bake in slow oven at 250 degrees for 2 hours or more.

Betty Switzer

Upon meeting Betty Switzer you experience a sense of connectedness like you've known her your entire life and can tell her anything. It is her personable nature that invites this comfort, and such was the case when I visited her in Fort Worth.

Every nook and cranny of her home offered an invitation to sit, but it was in the den she shared her admiration and love for her mother, Lillian Ruth Brannon Williamson. As I posed questions and watched her race through memories before answering, I noted that Betty Switzer's character is one of receptiveness and contemplation. Once she gathered her thoughts, words flowed, but it was in her not-too-quick-to-answer fashion that I came to know Betty Switzer.

Betty, the baby of the family, grew up in two worlds: the world of Fort Worth and the world of the country, and through the interweaving of those two worlds, groundwork was laid to provide her with a foundation of values. Values that led to a good life in marriage and church, civic, and social activities.

Betty Switzer

After moving to Temple in 1971, Betty pursued further involvement in the community. She and her husband taught Sunday school to high school juniors and seniors, and Betty sang in the choir. She was active in the Women's Club and to be connected with her children served as an officer in the local PTA and volunteered at their school. She also joined The Contemporaries—a ladies' support organization to the Cultural Activities Center which was Temple's local arts agency.

As a member of the Contemporaries Arts Education Committee she helped develop a program called "Hands On," which provided Temple elementary students first-hand involvement in the arts. She later served as president of the organization and was elected to two terms of service for the Cultural Activities Center.

When the children reached middle school age, she worked at their school. Then an opportunity arose to work as a staff member at the Cultural Activities Center and she accepted, serving as assistant to the director, director of volunteers, and staff coordinator for the Arts Education Program.

In 1982 Betty's husband was transferred to Austin, Texas, and she joined the staff of the Texas Assembly of Arts Councils (now known as the Texas Alliance for the Arts) as assistant director. She worked with local arts agencies in communities across the state, providing technical assistance and training opportunities to enhance organizational skills.

In 1984 Betty joined the staff of the Texas Commission on the Arts and currently holds the position of managing director of community development and rural services. Throughout her fifteen years with TAC, she has worked with community-based organizations in both urban and rural communities in developing new programs to address the specific needs of those communities. In her travels she has seen raw land grow into arts centers and museums and old buildings restored for arts facilities.

Throughout her years in arts administration, she has been recognized at the local, state, and national levels. For Betty, she proclaims there is no greater honor than to see an organization she has helped become a thriving, viable force in its community through the support of the agency and its funding. The year 1999 provided yet another unique situation for Betty when the TAC opened its first satellite office in Fort Worth, which provided her with two opportunities: to move to be close to her mother and care for her, and to be more closely involved in the arts in the North Texas area.

While Betty Switzer says that her work in the arts would not have been possible without the love and support of her husband of thirty-six years and the encouragement of her sons, she also gives credit to her mother, who taught her to believe that she could do anything she wanted if she wanted it badly enough.

Sarah Weddington

Lena Catherine Morrison Ragle

b. 1917

My mother did wonderful needlework, and my favorite piece is this angel. I like it not only because she used my favorite color blue, but more so because of the feeling that Mother was my angel who protected and looked over me.

MOTHER WAS DEVOTED to her family, children, and church, but clearly family was first. She was a preacher's wife, and there were parts of that role she enjoyed, like the people, and they loved her. She was always doing something for somebody else and had her own areas where she was the leader just as Daddy had the wider context of the church where he was clearly the leader.

She would have done anything for us. With a preacher husband and three kids, Mother had to manage frugally, but she constantly went without so we had opportunities to learn and be involved. Anytime I performed in the choir she'd try to be there, and she was a Cub Scout leader for my brother. She was always involved with church youth activities and made sure we had piano and art lessons.

She was always a support person, and if I needed someone to make something possible, I typically would go to her. I was certainly always grateful that Mother was devoted to us kids. I

Sarah Weddington and Catherine Ragle

Lena Catherine Morrison, high school senior, Carlsbad, New Mexico, 1935

Sarah Catherine Ragle, high school senior, Vernon, Texas, 1961

remember there was a time in junior high I wanted to be able to dance, and that was not something my father thought was a good thing. So because Mother was my champion, we reached a compromise that allowed me to go to square dancing if it was heavily supervised.

There were years I'm sure she hadn't had a new dress, but if it was a case of me or my siblings needing new clothes for some event, she made sure it happened. Now we might have had to pick the fabric and have somebody in the church sew it, but there were new clothes for us to do whatever we needed.

When I was head of the Future Homemakers of America in high school, Mother made sure I got to go to Chicago to the national meeting and that I got to go by train. She was the one to be sure I could do things like that. Then when I was getting my teaching certificate and decided during practice teaching I wanted to be a lawyer, that was okay. She never said that was inappropriate or unusual for a woman, even though there were only five women in my entry law-school class at the University of Texas in 1965. Instead I remember her saying, "Well, of course you can be a lawyer." Then she set up an appointment for me to talk to a church member who was a lawyer and helped organize my trip to Austin.

When I ran for political office, she came to Austin to volunteer; when I argued a case before the U.S. Supreme Court, she came to Washington, D.C., to cheer me on; when there was a move, she was there to help me get settled; she was eager to assist my busy life. You know in politics you have people who are called rainmakers because they bring in business or accomplish things. Well, Mother was the

Lena Catherine Morrison Ragle

rainmaker who made things happen, and indeed she was my champion.

Mother was really talented, and anything she decided to do basically she could do, but while a part of her soul was very confident and mentally curious about things, another part was somewhat sad. I think if she'd been born twenty-five years later she would have had a very different life. I think there were limits on her because so much was tied up in being a preacher's wife, and it was thought inappropriate at that time for a preacher's wife to work outside the home or church. So I think she would have enjoyed working but couldn't. I know she would have appreciated more income, not for herself but for her kids, because she wanted to be sure we had everything. You could say she accepted those limits because she loved and married my father, but I think she would have wanted a wider world within which to operate.

She was born too early to have those opportunities, but she realized her dreams through helping me achieve mine. Still I've always thought that if

I'd been born when she was and she'd been born when I was, we would have easily switched places. She certainly could have been a good lawyer. In later years she was able to get her masters in business administration and teach. But she in so many ways is characteristic of the really smart, hard-working, capable woman who achieved mostly through others instead of being able to do it on her own. Yet she never felt sorry for herself.

Mother died on January 27, 1993. After the Christmas holidays she began to feel ill and stayed home for about a week. Now Mother was one who if you said to her "How do you feel," she'd always say "Oh fine." She never complained, but she just wasn't getting better, and finally she told us she needed help, so we took her to the hospital. When she checked in they said she'd had a heart attack and would be okay, but then she went into a downward spiral, and they never could find an effective path of treatment. Mother was dead within a week.

When she passed away my brother and I were going through her things and found she had every report card and valentine I had gotten in the fifth or third or first grade. She had the Morrison family Bible from 1877, letters from her brother Bobby when he was in WW II, and my father's letters to her when he was in the Navy, and they were all organized and placed in this toy chest my father had built. So Mother was like the family curator.

When I think about Mother's legacy, I feel she produced three accomplished children. I think some of my strongest connections with Mother are that I got my determination, independence, and caring for others from her. But the thing I will always miss the most is how Mother enjoyed sharing in so much of what I was doing.

I thank Mother for her encouragement to explore the path I've been on because I've had such a good life and enjoyed so much that was shaped by her. I miss her, but I experience a bit of her in my activities daily and am grateful she was my mother. I thank Mother for who she was and what she gave to me: my roots and my wings!

Popcorn Balls

Popcorn balls were a big thing for us. Daddy and Mother both would be involved in this process that was a family ritual plus low-cost entertainment.

   5 qts. popped corn
   2 c. sugar
   1 ½ c. water
   ½ c. white corn syrup
   ⅓ tsp. salt
   1 tsp. vinegar
   1 Tbsp. vanilla

Put kernels in large pan. Boil water, sugar, and corn syrup without stirring to 260 degrees or until it cracks when tried in cold water.

Add vinegar, salt, and vanilla, and boil to 264 degrees. Pour slowly over corn, stirring and turning with spoon to coat each kernel evenly. Make into balls and let stand in cold place until brittle. Wrap in wax paper or baggies.

Mother's German Chocolate Cake

Mother's German chocolate cake was one of her best. I've tried to make it like her's through the years, but I've never been able to match it.

Grease and flour three 8- or 9-inch layer cake pans. Preheat oven to 350 degrees.

   1 pkg. Baker's German Sweet Chocolate
   ½ c. boiling water
   1 tsp. soda
   4 egg yolks, unbeaten
   ½ tsp. salt
   1 c. (2 sticks) butter
   1 c. buttermilk
   1 tsp. vanilla
   2½ c. sifted cake flour
   2 c. sugar
   4 egg whites

Melt chocolate in boiling water, cool. Cream butter and sugar until light and fluffy. Add egg yolks, one at a time, beating after each. Add chocolate and vanilla. Sift together salt, soda, and flour. Add alternately to buttermilk and chocolate mixtures, beating well after each addition. Beat until batter is smooth. Beat egg whites until stiff peaks form. Fold into batter. Pour into three 8- or 9-inch layer pans. Bake in moderate oven, 350 degrees for 30 to 40 minutes. Cool. Frost tops only.

Coconut Pecan Frosting

Combine 1 cup evaporated milk, 1 cup sugar, 3 egg yolks, ¼ pound of butter, and 1 teaspoon vanilla in a saucepan. Cook, stirring over medium heat until mixture thickens, about 12 minutes. Add about 1½ cups coconut and 1 cup chopped pecans. Beat until frosting is cool and thick enough to spread. Makes 2⅔ cups or enough to cover the tops of three 9-inch cake layers.

Broiled Grapefruit

You've got to try broiled grapefruit. It was something easy for a woman who had to organize three kids and something we could help with.

Use 2 grapefruits at room temperature. Cut in half, then cut thin slice from bottom for balance. Cut around every section close to the membrane. Fruit should be completely loosened from skin. Remove core from each half; dot grapefruit halves with butter.

Combine 2 tablespoons sugar with ½ teaspoon cinnamon; sprinkle on halves. Place on broiler rack or in shallow baking pan; broil 4 inches from heat for about 8 minutes or till heated through and bubbling. Garnish with stemmed maraschino cherries, if desired. Serves 4.

Mother's Corn Bread

1 c. Aunt Jemima's yellow cornmeal
1 c. flour
4 tsp. baking powder
¼ c. soft shortening (or Wesson oil)
¼ c. sugar
1 egg
½ tsp. salt
1 c. milk

Put cornmeal, flour, sugar, salt, and baking powder in bowl. Add egg, milk, and oil. Beat until smooth, about 1 minute. Don't over beat. Bake in greased 8-inch square pan or greased muffin pans in oven at 400 degrees for 20-25 minutes. If batter is stiff, add a little more milk or oil.

Sarah Weddington

Sarah Weddington

Within walking distance from the hurry-scurry activity of Austin's downtown district sits an older neighborhood rife with turn-of-the-century wooden and limestone houses that has been revitalized and within which stands the office of Sarah Weddington.

The office decor and design directly reflects the spirit of Ms. Weddington—confident and polished, comfortable and proud. In the narrow hallway stand floor-to-ceiling bookshelves that hold law books and family albums, and while the law books are impressive, it is the family albums that command attention as each large notebook is meticulously organized to reflect and catalog the Ragle family legacies through photographs, mementos, and article clippings. And all carry the spirit of Sarah's mother, Lena Catherine Morrison Ragle.

During the interview we sat in Sarah's office at a round table atop which was displayed a shrine-like montage of items reflective of Sarah's mother—there were photographs, needlework, family albums, books, you name it. And using these visual reminders as springboards, Sarah talked about her mother's unfailing support, family devotion, and role as the family curator. But perhaps the clincher came when Sarah identified her mother as a rainmaker—a title given to people in politics who make things happen—and the old saying "like mother, like daughter" made all the more sense.

In her world Sarah Weddington is a rainmaker. She is a nationally known attorney and spokesperson on leadership and public issues. In 1972 she was the first Austin woman elected to the Texas House of Representatives. From there she went to Washington as general counsel for the U.S. Department of Agriculture. She served as assistant to President Jimmy

Carter, 1978 to 1981, and directed the administration's work on women's issues and appointments. Later she became the director of the State of Texas Office of State-Federal Relations and worked as chief lobbyist for Texas.

In 1973 she successfully argued before the U.S. Supreme Court the landmark *Roe v. Wade* case, typifying her work on issues affecting women. She is a member of the board of the Foundation for Women's Resources, which launched programs that encourage women to strive for leadership goals.

Her list of awards includes ones such as: Leadership America's Hummingbird award, 1998, for contributions toward the advancement of women's leadership; the Woman Who Dares award, 1993, presented by the National Council of Jewish Women; and the Woman of Distinction award, 1993, given at the National Conference for College Women Student Leaders.

Named by *Time Magazine* as one of the "Outstanding Young American Leaders," and by *Ladies Home Journal* with the "Woman of the Future" award, Sarah Weddington's impact is nationally recognized. Currently she instructs a course called "Leadership in America" as an adjunct associate professor at the University of Texas in Austin.

Indeed it is obvious that her mother is clearly present—present in beliefs that there are no inappropriate roles for women, present in the spirit that gave her daughter, Sarah Weddington, both roots and wings.

Judith Zaffirini

Texas senator; journalist

Nieves Consuelo Mogas Pappas

b. 1916

Mother taught us to value spirituality and family. She taught us the importance of strengthening ties at all times, never taking relationships for granted, and being responsible for our choices. That was her legacy.

Nieves Consuelo
Mogas Pappas

MOTHER'S FATHER DIED when she was a child in Laredo. He was killed, I believe, during the Mexican Revolution, but I don't know much because it was difficult for her to talk about. I do know she always got teary-eyed when they would play the song, "Oh, My Papa"; she just could not hear that without crying. And her mother, who was quite a beautiful woman, died when my mother was sixteen. Mother always talked about losing her, about the pain of losing both parents, and how she had to learn to cope with life and death.

Yet Mother personified the word lady in the most traditional context. She had a great sense for good manners, for etiquette, for making other people feel at home. She was ladylike in the way she conducted herself and the way she spoke. Her voice was soft, her movements slow, and her attire conservative. I feel comfortable in many different settings because Mother taught me how to demonstrate good manners at all times, and because that was important to her, it was important to me. And Mother was one of the gentlest persons I ever met. She considered herself strong because she was very much in control, but even though she considered herself strong, I also considered her gentle.

My first and most vivid memory I recall with my mother was her teaching me at the age of three to read. I remember she was sitting in her bedroom in a small chair by the door and had a book on her lap. I was crouched by her on the floor. It had killed me that my older sister Celita was learning to read and getting ready for first grade, and I wanted to learn to read.

So when I finally turned five I wanted to go to school with both of my older sisters. But first graders were expected to be six years old to begin school. Well, Mother told the monsignor I could read all of the first grade books and was ready for school, and he listened and agreed to let Sister Imelda, a first grade teacher, test me. When I got to her classroom, she handed me the last book from the first grade class, which I read without a single mistake, so they admitted me.

The next day I went to school then at noon came home with my sisters to eat lunch, but I announced that was the end of my education because I hated having to sit still in my chair. Instead of telling me I had to return, Mother said, "Fine. You can stay home and help me wash dishes and clean your sisters' clothes while they go off to school." She had me put on an apron and start washing dishes. Well, when I looked out the window and saw my sisters running off to school, I took off my apron and ran out after them. Like I said, Mother was gentle and strong.

One thing important to Mother was taking family trips. I remember one year we took a tour of Texas cities with one being Austin where we visited the state capital. Many years later, in 1986, after I was sworn in as a Texas Senator, she gave me a gift—a piece of glass—and with it a note explaining the paperweight was one of two things that had belonged to her father. That moved me that she wanted me to have it. Also in that note she recalled the last time she had been in the Texas capital—when our family had visited the Texas Legislature—and how little did she know then that the next time she would visit it, one of her daughters would be sworn in as a senator.

I keep coming back to Mother's strength, but that is a key quality of hers. One morning Mother was cooking breakfast and she called out to my sister Sara—whose bedroom was behind the kitchen—"Sara, breakfast is ready." No Sara. Again, "Sara, come eat breakfast." No Sara. Again, "Saaraaa, breakfast is ready." Finally she went to check and found Sara dead. So Mother went into a depression and had a deep, deep guilt because she felt if she had checked on Sara earlier she might have gotten help in time, or if she had known CPR she might have saved Sara. Even though neither was probable, Mother had this sense of guilt and did not cope well with Sara's death until the birth of my son in 1982. He was a new love and interest for my mother, and that's when she began finally to cope with the loss of Sara.

And Mother was very much in love with my father, so when he died she again had a difficult time coping with death. After his actual death, it was twenty minutes before the doctors could resuscitate him. When they did he began breathing, but there was no interaction and he was kept alive only by artificial means. Finally Mother decided to give permission to have the respirator turned off, and that was definitely one point where she showed great strength. Another was when the doctor suggested that the family step outside as they turned off the machine. But Mother turned and in a level voice said, "No, why don't the doctors step outside so the family can be with him." The doctors did, and we were all with him when he died.

Later when Mother died, what we heard over and over was she was not only beautiful physically but also spiritually. She was quite a devout Catholic who prayed daily. She had a ritual where she would kneel on her side of the bed by the pillow and pray a rosary, then she would move down,

Senator Judith Zaffirini, son, husband, mother, Nieves Consuelo Mogas Pappas, and father
Photo courtesy of Texas Senate

kneel, and say another rosary. So she prayed rosaries around the entire bed every night.

Well, after her death we were cleaning out her room and I found in her Bible an essay I had written about her when I was in an eleventh grade religion class. Obviously Mother read it quite regularly since she kept it in her Bible, but I was so shocked to find that she still had it. Listen to some of the things I wrote:

I am sorry to say that I usually take the wonderful gifts we human beings are given by you, dear God, for granted.... Therefore, today I would like to thank you in a very special manner for the wonderful woman that you gave me as my mother. My mother is charitable to all. Any beggar who comes to our house does not leave until he has been fed and given some food to take with him.... She is always ready to give of her free time to help someone.... Whenever I think of the Blessed Mother I tend to picture her as looking somewhat like my mother. I guess this is because I love, admire, and respect her very much.... Thank-you, dear God, for giving me my mother.... When you created her you created a child who would grow up into one of your most faithful servants.

Puerco Adobado

(Pork in Red Chili Sauce)

> 4 pork shoulder roasts (approximately 26 lbs.)
> Pepper
> Unseasoned meat tenderizer
> Flour
> 4 oz. La India chili powder (no spices)

Preheat oven to 400 degrees. Wash meat and sprinkle all over with pepper and tenderizer. Sift flour on all sides and pat with hands. Bake uncovered (to sear) for 30 minutes. Lower temperature to 300 degrees and bake <u>covered</u> for 30-45 minutes. Drain fat or transfer meat without fat to another roasting pan. Dissolve chili powder in 5 cups water and pour over meat. Bake at 300 degrees for 3-4 hours (<u>covered</u>), basting every 30 minutes. (Or, preferably, bake at 275 degrees for 4-5 hours.) Bake until meat is so tender it comes apart with forks. Serve in chafing dish with margarita buns (miniature hamburger buns) or with warm tortillas.

This recipe was adapted for parties by my sister, Celita Borchers.

Scotch Shortbread

2¼ c. flour
¼ tsp. baking powder
I c. butter at room temperature
½ c. plus I Tbsp. sugar

Cream butter well, gradually adding sugar while creaming. Sift flour before measuring. Resift twice with baking powder. Stir flour into butter mixture in two or three portions, mixing until smooth after each addition. Knead a few times to blend well.

Place small balls (about ¼" in diameter) in 6 x 7 rows on baking sheets. Flatten each with ball of your palm. Bake at 325 degrees for 18-20 minutes or until a very delicate color. While hot, roll cookies in a sugar-cinnamon mixture and place on rack to cool.

Makes approximately 100 cookies.

The original recipe, from my late sister Sara Pappas, called for rolling out the dough on a lightly floured pastry cloth to a ¼" thickness, then cutting it into diamonds or with cookie cutters.

Italian Spaghetti

This recipe has been in the Zaffirini family for years. I got it from my mother-in-law, Mrs. R. G. Zaffirini Sr., who got it from her father-in-law, Rodolfo Zaffirini, who developed the recipe. My husband and I prepare this spaghetti together. He has adapted it to make 2½ times as much, using 15 pounds of boneless roast. We serve it with Italian salad and buttered garlic bread.

6 lb. lean roast (Pike's Peak is acceptable), boneless
I can Italian tomato paste
4 strained tomatoes
5 garlic pods
4 bacon slices
½ c. chopped onion

3 carrots (each cut into 4 pieces)
2 slices lemon peel
1 c. parsley
6 oz. red wine
2 bay leaves
Allspice, salt and pepper, olive oil, and corn oil
2 pkgs. spaghetti
Parmesan cheese

Cut meat into 2-inch cubes and sprinkle with salt, pepper, and allspice. Set aside. Combine enough olive oil and corn oil in a large Mexican cazuela to fry garlic, onion, and bacon. Add parsley, lemon peel, bay leaves, and carrots. Brown meat in mixture. Add wine, cover and simmer for 5 minutes. Add tomato paste and tomatoes.

Fill cazuela with enough water to boil slowly, about 3 hours. When meat sauce is cooked, boil spaghetti and add to sauce. Top each serving with Parmesan cheese. Serves 12 adults or 8 Italians.

Judith Zaffirini

A little before seven o'clock in the morning, I strode along a sidewalk that threaded an immaculately kept lawn and led to the Texas State Capitol. In the winter air my breath grew visible. Passing only two other people, I realized why Judith Zaffirini begins her day at an early hour, for in the sanctity of dawn is a reverence that elicits a calm spirit, a clear mind.

Inside I crossed the marble floor, which carried echoes of my footsteps to the far reaches of the ceiling. Once I arrived at Ms. Zaffirini's office, her gracious staff members greeted me then showed me to her office where I waited as she attended to last-minute business. The space blended formal architecture with personal touches.

Soon Ms. Zaffirini put aside her senatorial duties and talked about her mother—Nieves Consuelo Mogas Pappas. During Judith's accolades a statement cemented itself into my memory when she read from a handwritten essay found in the family Bible upon her mother's death. Her essay brimmed with adoration and thankfulness for her mother as she expressed her belief that when God created her mother he "created a child who would grow up into one of your most faithful servants." And it was this commonality—of both mother and daughter being faithful servants—that surfaced during the interview.

Judith graduated from the University of Texas in Austin with bachelor of science, master of arts, and Ph.D. degrees. Her work includes thirteen years of teaching and more than twenty years of public speaking. Through Zaffirini Communications, she provides consulting, workshops, one-on-one coaching, and keynote addresses. A distinguished communicator, educator, and leader, Judith has been honored by notable Texas associations for work in journalism and public service, and recognized repeatedly for publications, speeches, and public relations campaigns.

Senator Judith Zaffirini, 76th Legislature
Photo courtesy of Texas Senate

She also carries her duties and devotion to public service into the political arena. In 1986 she was elected senator, representing the 21st Senatorial District, and re-elected in 1996. She is the first Hispanic woman to serve as a Texas senator, President Pro Tempore of the Texas Senate, and Texas Governor for a Day. She is the senior senator from the border area and Bexar County and has been reappointed for three consecutive terms as chair of the Senate Health and Human Services Committee. Her senate committee works include: Committee on Finance and Education, Human Services Committee, Committee on Education, and Special Committee on Border Affairs to name a few.

She is the only senator with a career-long, one hundred percent attendance and voting record, and the bills she has sponsored number in the hundreds. To honor this powerhouse of civic duty, Senator Zaffirini has received more than three hundred fifty awards.

Beyond this, Judith Zaffirini is a wife and mother as well as a devout Catholic. It's quite appropriate that in her South Texas district she is referred to as *la patrona,* which translated offers two meanings: *boss lady* or *patron saint*. Easily, Judith Zaffirini is a formidable woman whose work ethic and compassion earn her rights to both nuances of the word.

Creating Your Own Mother's Journal

Tips on recording personal reflections about your mother:

- make or buy a special notebook
- use different colored ink pens, markers, pencils
- carry the journal at all times
- find a special location (or several) to record thoughts
- copy favorite photos of your mother and paste them into the journal for inspiration
- contact people who know your mother and ask them to write about their favorite memories/stories of your mother; put letters into journal
- if your mother is still living, ask her to fill in details; consider recording your mother as she relates information
- copy the following reflection topics onto separate pieces of paper, fold them, put them in a jar, and randomly select topics to write about in your journal

1. If you could freeze-frame one image of your mother using her hands, what would that image be?

2. What story would evolve from that mental snapshot of your mother using her hands? What emotions are tied in with that story? What life lessons are tied into it?

3. What is the single most positive quality you associate with your mother? Why? (i.e., trust, joy, spontaneity, patience, heroism, courage, creativity, etc.)

4. How (if at all) are you like your mother? What is the strongest connection you share with her?

5. Does the saying "The apple doesn't fall far from the tree" apply to your connection with your mother?

6. What pieces of advice can you recall hearing from your mother?

7. If you were to describe your mother in terms of a figurehead, an icon, who or what would she be? Why?

8. What are the most prominent positive "identities" you associate with your mother? (i.e., diplomat, caretaker, artist, survivor, teacher, warrior, scientist, etc.)

9. What one gift/present did your mother ever give you that means the most? Why?

10. What one gift/present did you ever give to your mother that meant the most to you? Why?

11. Describe your favorite shared adventure or time spent with your mother during your childhood, your teens, your adulthood.

12. When (if ever) was the first time you thought of your mother as a peer? Describe that time.

13. How would you describe your mother's soul? Her spirit?

14. What superstition(s) does your mother have? What stories go with it?

15. What are some of the special letters, notes, or cards you've received from your mother? What made them special?

16. What is your mother's favorite food? Make a list of different mother occasions that involve that food. Select one occasion from that list and write about it—sensory details, date, place, memories, etc.

17. What are some beliefs your mother has that have helped her get through life? Explore where she might have gained those beliefs and why they helped her.

18. What do you know about your mother's childhood home(s)? Where were they?

19. What special stories go along with your mother's childhood home(s)? Which home was her favorite and why?

20. What favorite story has your mother told about her own mom?

21. What feelings do you experience when you hold one of your mother's letters in your hands and reread it?

22. What people have been important to your mother? What were their names? How did she know them? Why were they important?

23. What event(s) were special to your mother? Why?

24. What is the figurative legacy your mother is leaving the family, the community, the universe, YOU?

25. What is your mother's favorite music? Musician? Instrument? Write about all of the mother memories you can associate with each.

26. Write about the favorite game your mother played with you when you were little.

27. Write about the aromas you associate with your mother.

28. If you were to associate a color with your mother, what would it be and why?

29. When you think back on your mother what do you realize about her life that you didn't realize when you were younger?

30. Write about the mother foods you associate with comfort.

31. Write about the mother rules of the house while growing up.

32. Write a note to your mother thanking her for the various things she does/did for you.

33. Make a list of twelve things you like/love about your mother.

34. Write a list of 25 sentences that all begin with the words "Mother is " Write insightful and interesting things about her.

35. What is the one (or more) thing you regret not having told your mother?

Recipe Index by Chapter

Susie Kelly Flatau is available for speaking engagements (conferences, seminars, book & literary clubs, organizations, etc.), book signings, and adult creative writing workshops that explore the stories and legacies connected with one's life.
To contact Susie Kelly Flatau, please write: P.O. Box 92975, Austin, TX 78709-2975.

Other books from

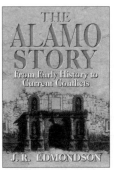

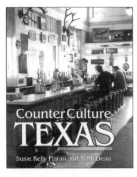

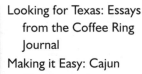

Republic of Texas Press